NEW ENGLAND
SEA
GLASS

NEW ENGLAND
SEA
GLASS

A VIBRANT HISTORY

ROXIE J. ZWICKER

THE
History
PRESS

Published by The History Press
Charleston, SC
www.historypress.com

First published 2024

Manufactured in the United States

ISBN 9781467156004

Library of Congress Control Number: 2024931851

To the "First Lady of Light," Connie Small, the Lighthouse Keeper's Wife—it was an honor to have known you, and I will never forget your stories of beachcombing in the shadows of many a lighthouse. Your light will always shine bright.

CONTENTS

INTRODUCTION

The sea, once it casts its spell, holds one in its net of wonder forever.
—*Jacques Yves Cousteau*

Captivating, mysterious, romantic—how does one describe the alluring attraction to the sea? Ever since I was young, I have found the sea to be entrancing, and I had always hoped that one day I would live close enough where I could visit as often as I wanted. When I was a teenager, I used to listen to cassette recordings of ocean waves as I fell asleep. Next to my bed was a corked glass jar with an assortment of beach-found treasures, along with sand I collected from my favorite beaches. Somehow, I knew that I could never be far away from the ocean. It never mattered what time of year it was or how cold it was; I made the most of every opportunity to escape to the beach, and I would stay there as long as I could, after the sun went down and sometimes until the moon came up.

In my early twenties, I moved to Cape Cod, Massachusetts, for a short time, and I truly thought it was paradise with historic sea captains' homes and quaint villages surrounded by salt marshes and so much incredible maritime history. I remember being awestruck when I viewed the expansive ocean beyond the rolling sand dunes of the Provincelands, which some locals call the "Old Cape." I would walk the long trails past "kettle holes" (ponds that were formed by leftover ice from moving and melting glaciers) and craggy pitch pines to the sandy shore of the beach. I was blissfully content just to sit down and pick through the seashells while listening to the symphony of

The author on one of her early sea glass adventures on Cape Cod.

waves. On a late afternoon one day, while sorting piles of colorful shells, I noticed a little sparkle, and as I picked it up and turned it in the sunlight, I marveled at the little jewel. I didn't know where it came from or what it was; I just knew it was something special. I had discovered my first piece of sea glass, and I wondered what its story was. I brought it home and put it in a glass dish on top of the stereo stand in my room, where my most treasured keepsakes were displayed. As time went on, I had a collection of sparkling sea-washed gems, and with each one, I felt so lucky to have found it.

The discovery of sea glass led me on adventures not only on beaches but also through the pages of books about lighthouses, seafarers, storms and ships. My imagination created the pictures and the scenes in my mind of the tales I had read about while I would walk the beach. I would look longingly at the deep blue horizon with a handful of sea glass rolling through my fingers and feel a tangible connection to history. I soon added pieces of found pottery along with colored and textured sea glass that had tumbled onto the shore. I felt like I had a mini museum of treasures, and I could tell you about each place I found them and what the sea was like that day. Some days when I was beachcombing, I felt like I had the whole beach to myself. I discovered that I could visit the same location several times and it was never the same beach twice. There were many trips to the beach when I would go home empty-handed, but that never mattered; I had still spent the day at the beach, and oftentimes that was just enough for me.

It's been many years since those first pieces of sea glass made it home in my sandy pockets, and I have achieved decorating an entire room with my sea-found treasures after many, many years. Some sea glass I have in jars with labels that have the beach names written on them. Certain favorite pieces are displayed in antique bottles or jars with lights around them so I can enjoy seeing their true colors. They continue to bring me joy, and sometimes I'll open one of the bottles and look at each piece again, holding it up to the light or feeling its smooth texture between my fingers, and it will bring me right back.

You'll still find me on the beach, breathing out my worries on an outgoing tide and breathing in the fresh, positive energy of an incoming tide. My eyes delight at full-moon light ladders that appear in the ocean waves on very special nights. I am often the last one to leave my favorite seaside park in my favorite neighborhood. As I drive away from the shore, a piece of sea glass in my pocket connects me to the past and is an assurance that I will return to the sea once again to discover what treasures await me upon my return.

CHAPTER 1

WHAT IS SEA GLASS?

Naturally formed sea glass comes from discarded, dropped and washed-away pieces of glass that have been tossed, turned and broken by the waves. Frosting or sugaring of the surface of the glass is produced in part by high pH levels, which is based on the acidity that is present in the salt water. The presence of lime, which is calcium oxides and hydroxides, in the glass is a factor as well. The geology of the beach is very important in the creation of sea glass, as the sand, pebbles and rocks act like a natural sanding tumbler to smooth the surface and shape of the glass. The power of the sea, waves and wind also keeps the glass tumbling and moving closer to the shore. Once the glass has been broken up from the original object that it was, the smaller pieces are very light and are tossed about quite easily.

One of the most important ingredients in creating sea glass is time. It can take ten to twenty years for sea glass to start to form, based on the conditions of the location it's in. Fifty or more years of tumbling in the surf can break down thicker and larger pieces to an almost smooth texture. Some pieces of sea glass have been proven to be hundreds of years old, based on their color and identification; the natural process of creating sea glass cannot be rushed or duplicated by hand. When examining some pieces of sea glass up close, the pits are visible along with "c" marks on the surface, which is a good indicator that the glass has been getting conditioned for quite some time.

Colorful glass can be easy to spot in between stones and pebbles along the shore. Clear or white glass can be difficult to spot when it's wet. Even more difficult, the weathering on dark-colored glass can render it to look like beach stones, and most pieces are easily overlooked when beachcombing. Some sea glass becomes so weathered that it eventually returns to its original state of sand. It is estimated that glass will take thousands of years to break down completely. Some people refer to sea glass as mermaid tears or mermaid treasure from dreamy stories in old folktales.

CHAPTER 2

COLLECTING HISTORY
AMONG THE WAVES

L et's explore the many ways in which glass ends up in the sea to begin with. When I moved to the southern Maine coast years ago, I couldn't believe my good fortune of having the opportunity to be at the ocean's edge within a quick five- to ten-minute drive to the nearest beach. I was drawn to the area not only because of the beauty of the ocean but because of the incredible history and amazing architecture that I discovered here as well. One of the first things I decided to do was get involved with our local lighthouse preservation group, which was a wonderful way to connect with the local community and spend time by the ocean. It wasn't long before I found myself beachcombing underneath the walkways to the lighthouse. I was picking up handfuls of sea pottery and beach glass, and I felt like I was picking up pieces of history. What were these pieces originally before the waves and tides broke them down into these little gems? My imagination ran wild, and if I closed my eyes, I could see the ships gliding across the waves toward me or the couple who had a romantic Victorian picnic with ornate teacups on the shore. I went to the library and read books and newspaper articles on local maritime happenings, storms and disasters going back to the seventeenth century, and somehow, I felt a tangible connection to that past I could really appreciate. Initially, I never thought what I was picking up was trash; rather, I felt like an archaeologist uncovering layers of the past, and I always wanted to know more about what I was finding and how it got there.

The storms in New England are legendary, from swift-moving hurricanes to snow-heavy blizzards. Some people will use those experiences to mark time frames in the telling of the history of a location. The path of each storm has changed the landscape with severe wind, waves, flooding and snow destroying sections of coastal communities, washing homes and buildings into the sea. Entire fishing fleets and countless boats have been washed away over the years. Erosion from these storms has permanently opened and closed harbors and access to some of the islands off the coast. So much of New England has been lost into the ocean by weather calamities over its history.

New England is also home to over 5,400 known shipwrecks, and new discoveries are being made each year. Some of those discoveries come to light because of explorations by curious folks. Treasure hunters and divers have found pieces of history that in many cases were hidden for centuries, embedded in the ocean floor or in the thickly packed sand beaches. The famous pirate ship the *Whydah*, captained by Black Sam Bellamy, which wrecked off Cape Cod in 1717, was finally found in 1984 with much of its treasure still intact. Ships like the *Whydah*, along with their lost cargo and artifacts, keep their secrets hidden so many fathoms down.

I had the pleasure of interviewing scuba diver Dick Scott, who is the owner of Portsmouth Scuba in Portsmouth, New Hampshire. He explained his experiences and discoveries from eight hundred dives over the past sixteen years, including the southern Maine and New Hampshire coast area. He explained:

> *My biggest regret in life is not diving sooner. It was one of those things I always wanted to do. Beyond the wildlife and stuff like that, it is just awesome to see underwater and its natural environment. It's very unique every time you go out there, you never know what you're going to find. I have a bottle that when I found it, I didn't have to dig for it or anything. We had a recent storm and the storm had washed away the mud and the silt from it. It was sitting there like it had just been dropped yesterday. Once you find something, it's really cool when you go back and research it. This Dr. Haynes bottle I found is from Providence, Rhode Island, the company was around in 1883. When you find a piece like that, it's like finding a piece of history; it's so awesome. One of the sailors on a ship would have got it when they were in Providence, and they sailed up to Portsmouth. When I searched for it, I discovered since it has balsam in it, it would have been used for pain relief.*
>
> *When I first started [diving], I had a guy tell me, "Oh, I always find marbles." I'm like, you always find marbles, and soon after, I started*

The folks at Portsmouth Scuba have a wonderful collection of sea glass and artifacts found in the waters of southern Maine and New Hampshire.

finding them. So, it's funny. Marbles, bottles, chamber pots. One of my exciting finds was when I found a pipe. The sailors would have their pipes and then break off the end zone and throw it in the water. I have a full pipe in my shop. Sometimes it's after a storm or sometimes the luck of the draw. You start looking for things that aren't natural, like a pipe. You see that straight line and you start looking at it, because it has some creation to it. To think that some of this stuff is almost three hundred years old. It's just amazing to see. We have a couple of clay pots that were found. One of them, unfortunately, when they tried to bring it up, basically split in half. But some of it has been down there so long once you bring it out of the water it just breaks.

I dive anywhere from twenty feet to sixty or seventy feet. It gets murky. So, if you just skim the surface and keep an eye out. When I found the chamber pot, it was sticking up, and I was like, oh, it's a plate. So, I brushed it off and it wasn't lifting. I'm kind of holding on to it and wiping away, and the next thing I know, I kind of pull it out. It was almost like pulling a boot out of the mud as you walked out.

Left: This nineteenth-century chamber pot was embedded at the bottom of the Piscataqua River in Portsmouth, New Hampshire.

Right: This terrific onion bottle dates back to the seventeenth or eighteenth century, and its uneven surface holds the key to its age.

A typical dive is about forty minutes; visibility is good at twenty feet. If I start going down thirty, forty feet here in our New Hampshire waters, it gets pretty dark. So, you stay off the bottom until you dig something up. But once you dig it up, now it's, where do I put it? Because if for some reason something happened and you need to go up and you have all this stuff attached to you; it could drag you down. Smaller things like marbles, the bottle, I put them in my pockets.

The oldest piece I have sitting in my shop is a red clay pipe. The person that found it had someone look at it, and they were like, there's no way there should have been red clay up here. That's probably from the 1600s. I also found a couple of pieces of plates at the Nubble Lighthouse in York, Maine. I have to be really careful because it gets really narrow between the lighthouse and the point. If the tide is coming in or out, it'll actually suck you through there. I have accidentally gotten swept through there once. Oh man! It was actually kind of fun because you're riding the current, but scary. But then when you get out to the other side, there's not as much good stuff to see. So, if you look at the left side of the lighthouse, that's really the good area to go diving.

The channel between Nubble Lighthouse and Sohier Park in York, Maine, is a favorite of local divers.

His advice if you are looking to add diving to your beachcombing adventures: "Go with a guide that knows the area. That way when you start you can see what to look out for, including the hazards of the area. When I go diving my tools are just my light and my hands. I've had good enough luck finding stuff."

A series of discoveries in an area of the New Hampshire seacoast known as Hart's Cove at the entrance to the Piscataqua River alludes to the incredible number of treasures hiding in the seabed among the sea life and abandoned lobster traps. Layers of discoveries were made from twelve inches to eight feet down in the silt and sand over the span of twenty years by Ray Demers and his son John. In the 1960s, while diving for scallops, they discovered an antique cannon, which prompted further explorations. With a unique technique of moving the sand and silt with blasts of air, they discovered and excavated over one thousand artifacts dating back to the 1600s. The

artifacts came from around the world and gave a rare and unique window on the shipping trade along the seacoast. A variety of discoveries was traced to the west coast of England. Some of the items recovered were determined to come from shipwrecks, while others were attributed to being tossed overboard from ships.

Many of the early settlers in the area were faithful to the British Crown and did not support the efforts of the Puritans who were trying to get a foothold in the region. The ships moving in and out of the port were controlled by wealthy merchants who made untold fortunes at sea. It is fascinating to chart the evolution of the port through the items that were found by the Demers family. This incredibly significant collection of historic finds was donated to the New Castle Historical Society and is an absolute treasure to the history of not only the local community but also the state of New Hampshire. Extensive research is currently being conducted on the artifacts by several museums and organizations.

A curious window on the world of traded goods was made when a remarkable discovery happened in 1974 during an excavation at the Narbonne House in Salem, Massachusetts. The house, which was built in 1675, is part of the National Park Service and is a designated historic site.

Opposite: Rum bottles and wine bottles from the seventeenth and eighteenth centuries that are part of the Demers collection that was donated to the New Castle Historical Society.

Above: Countless antique bottle necks were excavated from shipwrecks along the shores of New Hampshire by divers Ray and John Demers.

Kitchenware fragments and dishware along with glassware and livestock bones were pulled up from shipwreck sites in New Hampshire.

The property was owned by Captain Stephen Phillips, who was a successful sea captain and merchant mariner during the eighteenth century. A trash pit was excavated, which was a glimpse into the goods being brought into Salem. Several thousand artifacts were unearthed, including shards of seventy-one vessels of glass. Bohemian glassware from Germany was identified, including stemmed wine glasses and tumblers. German glassware was less expensive than British ware but was still considered stylish. A large quantity of wine and rum bottles was also found in the pit, which also told the story of brewing and drinking during Salem's golden age. Beer and rum distilleries operated and prospered in Salem as early as the mid-seventeenth century. By 1773, fifteen purveyors in Salem were selling all sorts of spirits from St. Croix rum to cherry brandy.

Oftentimes cargo would be sold right off the ships at the docks. In advance of their arrival at port, captains would advertise their cargo and then announce the date, and it would be sold. Auctions were quite a popular way for a large amount of goods to be sold quickly and easily. Blue willow pattern chinaware was recorded to be a quite popular item, and bidding was often described as spirited. During the time of the American Revolution and the War of 1812, the English made a variety of decorative items that were popular, although wealthy Americans preferred French china. An abundance of English dishware can still be found in small fragments near the old dock sites in major New England ports.

Even gravestones have been claimed by the sea. In the clam flats of Ipswich, Massachusetts, a gravestone from 1879 washed ashore in 2023. In Cohasset, Massachusetts, 150 graves in a historic seaside cemetery were getting flooded by high tides. The gravestones had to be elevated, and a seawall was built in 2020 to keep them from washing away. Ironically, in seventeenth-century New England colonies, quarried stone slabs from England to be used as gravestones were used as ballast in ships. Some carved gravestones in the eighteenth and nineteenth centuries were shipped to ports up and down the coast. Small gravestone fragments have been known to wash ashore with partial names and dates from the coast of Maine all the way down to Rhode Island.

In this book, you will find that the artifacts that were once part of the evolution of New England's coastal cities or towns seem to have slipped just below the ocean waves. Bricks and stones from old houses and other structures are slowly breaking down little by little over time, tumbling into the harbors. Debris from fires and severe storms has floated off into the ocean or, sadly, in some cases was purposefully dumped, like after the great 1866 fire in Portland, Maine. Many trash dumps dotted the coastlines and were slowly leached into the ocean, polluting the environment but starting the glass on its way to becoming tumbled sea glass.

Over four hundred years of traded and exported goods have made their way into the waters too, and eventually they are rolling up onto the beaches. Shipwrecks are sometimes revealed after storms and then disappear beneath the sands when weather conditions change. Sea captains, sailors and travelers didn't often toss their trash into waste baskets; rather, things would get tossed over the sides of their vessels. For as long as man has been traversing the ocean, all sorts of things have fallen into it.

CHAPTER 3

BEACHCOMBING TIPS AND TECHNIQUES

One of the most important things to remember, whether you are starting your beachcombing journey or have been at it for many years, is to be patient when looking for sea glass. I have had countless trips to the beach when I've spent hours diligently searching and have left empty-handed. Yet there have been other times when I've just stepped into the parking lot of the beach and have seen shimmering nuggets of sea glass on the pavement that have been tossed ashore by the waves. A lot of folks get discouraged if they don't find anything, but remember, any day at the beach is a great day! Just because there may not be glass to collect after a couple of visits doesn't mean that there won't be a piece waiting for you on your next visit.

Some of the best times of year to go collecting in New England are early spring and winter, for several reasons. The most obvious reason is that the beaches are largely empty, and you might have the location all to yourself. Parking your car might be free, and finding a spot may also be a lot quicker. New England is known for its winter storms. Nor'easters can be accompanied by powerful wind gusts that drive the waves along the shore sky high. Storm surges can cause a lot of damage to coastal communities as the sea roars onto the land. Once the weather has safely subsided, you'll find some sea glass collectors bundled up and headed to the shore to be the first to comb the beach for the latest collection of sea debris that has been tossed ashore.

Tidepools are fantastic places to view sea life and find the occasional piece of sea glass.

Another key element in having successful sea glass–collecting experiences is knowing your tides. There are smartphone apps that are helpful for predicting the tides, or you can consult the website of the National Oceanic and Atmospheric Administration (NOAA). Tides work in direct response to the gravitational pulls of the moon and the sun. The tides combined with the current—which is largely driven by the shape of the land, wind and water temperature—move the shoreline and whatever ends up on it. Ideally, going to the beach as the waters approach low tide is a great idea because you will have more shore to explore. However, I have also had luck when the water is coming in after a high tide because the waves have shifted their push toward the shore. Keep in mind that because of their size, some beaches and locations disappear altogether as the tides approach the high mark, and you don't want to find yourself stranded.

One of the things that I believe a good beachcomber can develop is what I like to call sea glass eyes, and once you get the hang of it, it will feel like second nature. When you step onto a beach, slowly scan from one side to the other while standing in one spot. As you take in the terrain, you can see if it's stony, pebbly, sandy or rocky. Give your eyes a moment to adjust

Clear or white sea glass is practically invisible when below the waterline.

and then focus on the spaces between the rocks, shells or seaweed. Once you've focused on those spaces, it's easy to look over the beach with a scan of your eyes on the first pass. Because sea glass is so small, you may see only an edge of it sticking out, as the rest may be obscured under whatever else is on the beach.

Did you know that you can hear sea glass? As the flotsam and jetsam is pushed around with the tides, you can hear the pebbles and stones rolling in the water, and if you listen carefully, you can hear the slight high-pitched "tinkling" sound as the glass rolls around. Sometimes hearing a piece of glass faintly pinging off a nearby rock is like a siren's call to go explore that spot. Once you've spotted the glass, be sure to look carefully around the same spot, because oftentimes there might be another piece or two being tossed around with it.

Walking slowly along the beach with the sun behind you or over your shoulder can help illuminate the treasures on the beach as well. When the light hits the glass at an angle, the glass will stand out against the background. If you find yourself wandering the beach and the sun has gone down, you may notice that some people hunt for sea glass with a flashlight or headlamp. What is interesting about hunting for sea glass at night is that there are usually fewer people on the beach, and you can extend the hours of your treasure seeking.

If you are feeling particularly adventurous, you can also pack an ultraviolet flashlight in your bag and use that to search for and identify uranium sea glass on the beach. True uranium glass contains uranium oxide, which glassmakers would add to their process. The colors range from bright green to pale yellow, and it was produced from the 1830s to the 1950s. If you already have some sea glass in your collection, it is worth investing in a small ultraviolet flashlight and shining it on the pieces; you may already have a glowing treasure in your midst.

Putting the "combing" into beachcombing is a great way to get in touch with your inner archaeologist. If you've got the time, will and energy to put in a bit more effort to find sea glass and other beach treasures, you may be pleasantly surprised how quickly your collection will grow. Walking the tideline on the beach and sweeping with your foot or a stick is a great way to uncover another layer that someone else might just walk past. Be gentle

Glass bottle stoppers are on the bucket lists of many sea glass collectors.

while sweeping through the layers and uncover things slowly to reveal what might be hidden. A long-handled skimmer or strainer scoop is fantastic to sift through small areas and pick out even the smallest pieces that your eyes might miss. A strainer with at least a thirty-six-inch handle should serve you well. A small hand rake or garden rake is another easy way to move the surface around and make some discoveries. I remember one April I had gone to the beach, and there were these large piles of gravel in several places. I sat down and took my flower box rake and slowly combed the gravel, and much to my surprise, I ended up filling a plastic sandwich bag with sea glass, porcelain and pottery in about an hour and a half. Some of my finds that afternoon were the best discoveries of that year.

Mapping out a good day at the beach can be a great approach to logistically plan your visit. Looking at satellite maps online or nautical charts—if you've got an understanding of them—can be a great way to calculate and map out your next adventure. Seeing the expanse of the shore can help you find coves or secret spots to walk to on your next visit that you might not be aware of. Rocky edges of beaches or the paths along salt marshes can be surprising places to find sea glass. Glass is light and is tossed quite easily and sometimes can travel farther than you might realize. Please keep in mind to *always* be respectful of private property lines, no trespassing zones and conservation and preservation areas.

Dress appropriately, wear beach shoes, have gloves and be prepared for quick changes in the weather. There are many hazards to beachcombing, and you don't want an injury to ruin a good day at the beach. Some beaches were former dump sites, and there might still be hazardous items on the beach. Keeping a first aid kit in the car is a must because some glass is sharp and can even cut through gloves. Some sea glass collectors will even wear wading boots or overalls if they are going into the water, while others are content just walking on the sand; whatever you choose to do, always make smart decisions about protecting yourself with the right gear and clothing.

CHAPTER 4

MAINE

The scent of the fragrant pines, the tang of the salty sea
Will call us home.
—excerpt from the "State of Maine Song," the official song of Maine,
written in 1937 by Roger Vinton Snow

The spectacular coast of Maine truly expresses one of the reasons why Maine is known as "Vacationland." With nearly three thousand miles of coastline, the sea is intertwined with the state's past as well as the present. It has been suggested that the area we now know as Maine was visited by Vikings. Curious carved figures were discovered on the basaltic rocks on the shores of Machias. In 1979, researchers positively identified a piece of coin found at Blue Hill to be a genuine Norse or Viking coin. The coin was estimated to be more than nine hundred years old and is believed to be the oldest known European artifact found in North America. In 1497, John Cabot, an Italian explorer, was said to have explored the area while mapping trade routes, but no record of his actual route survives.

Modern-day explorers are still called to visit the Pine Tree State to see where the forest meets the sea. The rugged shore of this place offers vistas that seem to go on forever in panoramic views. A stress-free feeling is easily achieved, as there are still so many places to connect with the natural solitude here. Taking a harbor cruise and hopping off to explore one of Maine's many islands can be rewarding in many unexpected ways. A leisurely walk along a beach will offer the serenity of ocean waves, passing lobster boats, pleasure boats and the occasional historic vessel. You can go at your own pace, kayaking the seemingly endless shore and many inlets that make up the coast. There are so many places to pick up a piece of Maine's history being carried by the tides. What will you discover here?

Fort Popham

The first organized attempt at an English colony in what we now know as Maine was located at the mouth of the Kennebec River, near the current town of Phippsburg, in the summer of 1607. It was known as the Popham Colony. The settlers attempted to set up a trading post and even constructed the first ship that was built in the New World. However, all their efforts failed for a few reasons, including poor relations with the Native peoples, along with not finding enough natural goods and resources for them to send back to England. Faced with another harsh winter, the colony was abandoned one year later in 1608. Archaeological surveys and excavations have been extremely active in recent years around the area of the original settlement.

The Fort Popham state historic site is often cluttered with driftwood of all shapes and sizes, as well as sea glass.

Construction on Fort Popham along the Kennebec River began in 1861 to protect the shipbuilding facilities farther upriver in Bath. During World War I, the fort was quite busy with activity, and there were many tents pitched inside, along with soldier drills and guards stationed behind its walls. The fort was never fully completed and was purchased by the State of Maine in 1924. The six-acre site has expansive views across the river and lots of little pockets of the shore to explore. This is a terrific place to gather the abundant pieces of driftwood that get caught up in the rocks on the edges of the beach. While picking for sea glass may not always be by the handful, depending on the tide, the pieces I've discovered tend to be larger and more interesting than most places in the area. Parking is free on site, and there are even a few places to have a picnic lunch.

Kennebunkport

Kennebunkport was incorporated as a town on July 5, 1653, under its original name of Cape Porpoise. It is estimated that the first ship built here was an eighty-ton ship in 1755. More than 140 vessels were built in Kennebunkport in the nineteenth century. By 1888, boating on the river was deemed "one of the most enjoyable features of life at Kennebunkport," and by 1894, almost five hundred canoes operated on the river. In the twentieth century, the community became quite a destination for summer travelers and remains so today. Out on Walker Point is the Bush Estate, which served as the summer White House of George H.W. Bush, the forty-first president of the United States. First Lady Barbara Bush was a sea glass collector, and she was known for the admirable collection that she gathered on the family property.

Each spectacular ship built in Kennebunkport had a story to tell, and one of the spookier stories is still being told. The *Isidore* was a sturdy and seaworthy bark that weighed in at about 396 tons and was built in 1842. The men who had signed on to its maiden voyage described nightmares and premonitions of the ship being taken down by the waves in a storm, and one man even refused to go and instead hid in the woods the morning the ship was to set sail. As the boat was being launched down the ramp to meet the rising tide, it swayed from side to side, and a collective gasp could be heard from the crowd. The lean and slope of the ship led many watchers to believe that it wouldn't even make it to the sea. Despite the apparent

Kennebunkport is a fantastic place for a seaside adventure and is full of legends and lore.

concern, the *Isidore* held its own once it was fully afloat in the cold waters of the Kennebunk River. It was then moored to a wharf, ballasted and made ready for its maiden voyage to New Orleans. The north-northeast breeze slowly strengthened throughout the day.

The crew of fifteen was eerily quiet on the ship as it floated away on the tide. It was said that the loved ones of the crew wept out loud on the shore, many fearing the premonitions that had been mentioned in recent hours. As the afternoon progressed, the northeast winds began to increase, and a light snow began to fall. At sunset, the *Isidore* was seen just off Boon Island in nearby York, Maine. The waves began to intensify, with thirty-foot swells, and the snow was becoming blinding. By midnight, the storm had become a screeching gale with monstrous waves. The *Isidore* was clearly doomed. In the morning, the tragedy of the night was revealed along Avery's Cove in York, six miles west of Boon Island. The splintered ship washed ashore in pieces; the bow was visible but was covered in water. The ship's cargo of lumber littered the rocky shoreline. Some people believe Captain Foss may have made the decision to sail back to port, but it was too late.

About ten years after the wreck of the *Isidore*, tales of a phantom ship were told. Sightings of the phantom ship have been reported from Kennebunkport down to Rye, New Hampshire. It is described as sailing without any sound, with tattered sails and a crew on deck that just seems to stare off into the distance. When approached, it sails off into the mists and vanishes. Some mariners have reported that they have tried to throw a line to the ship, but it only turns and sails away. It is believed by some that the ship is still sailing, looking for the man who refused to fulfill his obligations to sail on *Isidore*'s maiden voyage. Others believe that it is a reminder of the perilous dangers of the coast during a storm. In 1912, the *Maine Sunday Telegram* recounted the story of the *Isidore* and included additional commentary regarding the ghost ship by reporter Chandler Briggs Allen:

> *The yarn of the Phantom Ship may be rejected as a product of superstitions and morbid imagination, it matters nothing. But even the hardest headed person must accept well-substantiated and incontrovertible facts, and there are enough to make one wonder if, after all, there might not be a grain of truth in the yarn the sailors used to tell.*

Colony Beach at the mouth of the harbor where the Kennebunk River empties into the Gulf of Maine has always been a choice collecting spot. The beach is rocky, and it is the perfect place to pick between the rocks

A thick piece of an aqua canning jar rests on top of the rocks in Kennebunkport.

and discover some larger pieces of sea glass, like Coke bottle and mason jar shards. Sky and weather watching is perfect from this vantage point with amazing and swift-moving cloud formations over the sea. It is believed that if you peer into the swirling sea mist just offshore, you can catch a glimpse of the phantom ship *Isidore* from the beach.

CAPE ELIZABETH

Cape Elizabeth is home to beautiful Crescent Beach at the edge of Casco Bay. The legend is that the veil between the worlds sometimes grows thin in this liminal space as the tidewaters of the Atlantic Ocean roll around your feet.

The tragically romantic tale is the story of the "ghost bride" of Cape Elizabeth, Lydia Carver. Lydia was one of seven children of Amos Carver, who had become a wealthy Portland businessman. Her family had moved to nearby Freeport from the Plymouth area of Massachusetts. Unfortunately, there are not many personal details known about Lydia herself or about the man she was supposed to marry. But what is certain is that her sad tale began in July 1807.

An excited twenty-three-year-old Lydia, along with twenty-one other people (mostly her bridal party), boarded the schooner *Charles* and set out to Boston to have her wedding gown fitted. The captain of the ship was Jacob Adams of Portland, who had brought along his wife.

On Sunday, July 12, the schooner sailed off from Boston to complete the overnight trip back to Portland. It was said to be a bright and sunny summer day as the *Charles* made good time on the return journey. As the schooner approached Richmond's Island, just before midnight, a severe gale seemed to blow in out of nowhere, and tragedy seemed imminent. The Atlantic Ocean roared, and towering waves overcame the *Charles*. The swells caused the schooner to strike Watt's Ledge, fifty feet offshore from Richmond's Island. The schooner tipped over onto its side, and the bottom was ripped out.

The passengers on the *Charles* faced their doom in the cold ocean waters as the waves washed over the wrecked schooner. Some of the passengers attempted to cling to the ship's rigging; however, they were no match for the stormy sea. Captain Adams and three other men attempted to reach the shore of Richmond's Island. Frantic cries from Adams's wife called him back to the ship, and as he attempted to return to her, the waves carried him off to a watery grave.

Those who tried to find a way to hold on to the remains of the schooner were forced into the sea as the *Charles* broke apart during the late-night hours. When the storm passed and the morning sun appeared, a devastating scene revealed itself on nearby Crescent Beach. The body of Lydia Carver had washed ashore, and next to her was her trunk, holding her never-to-be-worn bridal gown. In all, sixteen people perished that fateful July night.

The bodies of the captain and his wife were also recovered, and they were buried at the Eastern Cemetery in Portland. Lydia's body was buried at a little countryside burial ground overlooking Crescent Beach.

Among the fragrant beach roses, the gravestone for Lydia tells the very dramatic story:

> *Sacred to the memory of*
> *Miss Lydia Carter*
> *daut'r of Mr Amos Carter of Freeport*
> *AE 21 who with 15 other unfortunate*
> *passengers male and female perished*
> *in the merciless waves by the shipwreck*
> *of the schooner* Charles *Capt. Jacob Adams*
> *bound from Boston to Portland*
> *on a reef of rocks near the shore of*
> *Richmond's Island on Sunday night*
> *July 12, 1807*

There are about twenty gravestones in the burial ground, some newer than the stone for Lydia. It is Lydia's stone that seems to be in the best condition, as it is totally legible. I learned about Lydia's story when I received a call some years back from the nearby Inn by the Sea, which originally opened in 1982. There were a surprising number of ghost stories coming from the inn regarding sightings of Lydia wearing her white wedding gown. During one visit to the inn, I met an older woman from the Cape Elizabeth Historical Society who had quite a ghost story to share. She told me that in the 1960s, her daughter caught a glimpse of Lydia on nearby Route 77. There are lush meadows and small forested areas along this very scenic but typically quiet road that leads past the inn. I was told that as the young woman was traveling in her car, she noticed two figures standing by the side of the road. As the woman approached, she discovered a lady wearing a long white wedding gown standing silently, resting her hand on a female deer that stood completely still at her side. The woman in the gown made eye contact with the traveler on Route 77, and then as the car passed, she vanished; a look in the rearview mirror revealed that there was no one there. The woman's daughter was quite certain that she had seen the ghost of Lydia Carver that night.

The people who worked at the Inn by the Sea believed that Lydia would appear from time to time in the mirrors in the hotel and that she took an occasional ride on their elevator. There is a portrait of Lydia Carver that hangs in the inn, and oddly enough, no one knows where it came from or how it got there—it was just always there. There were tales from the restaurant about place settings and dishes being moved around without explanation. Staff also believed that the spirit of Lydia might be taking care of her gravestone, which might explain why it's always in such spotless condition. There are many stories and sightings of Lydia's spirit walking on nearby Crescent Beach as well. Beachcombers have said that a strange fog will roll in over Richmond's Island and you can see the masts of a wrecked ship sticking out of the fog. Visitors to the beach have reported that on some evenings, you can hear a tremendous crash followed by screams echoing from the Watt's Ledge area. Does the spirit of Lydia Carver still walk Crescent Beach? You might find yourself looking over your shoulder as you pick up a small treasure that might connect you to the sorrowful tale of the ghost bride.

Peaks Island, Casco Bay

Peaks Island in Casco Bay is just 762 acres and is under the jurisdiction of Portland, Maine. There are approximately one thousand full-time residents on the island. Peaks Island was the traditional territory of the Wabanaki and was colonized by Europeans in the mid-seventeenth century. During the 1820s, the first ferries made their way out to Peaks Island, and by the 1850s, there were two hotels on the island. During the great gale of September 8, 1869, the schooner *Helen Eliza Mass* was driven ashore in the darkness onto the rocks on the outside of the island. The crew tried to swim to safety, but of the twelve aboard, only one man, Charles Jordan of Rockport, Massachusetts, succeeded in reaching the shore alive. Ten bodies were recovered, and the captain's body was found in a cove on the harbor side of the island. The ship was ground to pieces on the rocks and strewn along the shore. Longfellow, in his poem "The Wreck of the *Hesperus*," vividly describes this wreck on Peaks Island:

> *Down came the storm and smote amain*
> *The vessel in its strength;*
> *She shuddered and paused like a frightened steed,*
> *Then leaped her cable's length.*
> *The breakers were right beneath her bows,*
> *She drifted a dreary wreck,*
> *And a whooping billow swept the crew*
> *Like icicles from her deck.*

The approach to the Forest City Ferry Landing on Peaks Island dates back to the 1880s.

By the turn of the twentieth century, there were three theaters, a boardwalk, summer cottages and sixteen hotels on the island. People came from all over the country to what became known as the Coney Island of Maine. As soon as people stepped off the boats, they could find the supplies they needed for their visit. The C. Way and Company was located right on the landing, and any remedies or medications that were needed could be obtained right at the shoreline. In the summer, dozens of steamboats brought in people to crowded amusements, including a Ferris wheel and hot air balloon rides.

The 1930s saw change coming to the island, as it was the time of the Great Depression. People were traveling by car, and a few fires plagued the island, destroying seventeen houses, the Gem Theater and even some of the amusements. The Greenwood Garden Beer House served root

An area known as the "rubble zone" on the east side of Peaks Island is an ideal place to find cairns, driftwood sculptures and unusual rocks.

beer and ginger beer, although according to legend, they may have secretly sold and served alcoholic beer. During World War II, there was a two-hundred-acre army base built on the island, which brought nearly one thousand military personnel to Peaks. Battery Steele, constructed on Peaks in 1942, is one of the largest gun battery structures ever built. There are three entrances through the woodland trails to find its remains. In May 1957, after the war ended and the military left the island, a fire swept across Peaks Island for three days. The broken glass that was left behind from some of the abandoned military buildings ignited the tall grass, and three hundred acres of the island were destroyed.

Because Peaks Island has seen so many visitors over the years and because of all the fires, there is a bit of debris floating around the island. Sea glass, porcelain bits and pottery finds can be discovered at Sandy Beach, which is located on the southwest part of the island. You can also kayak out to Catnip Island for more terrific beachcombing. Centennial Beach is located near City Point off Island Avenue and is a terrific place to sift through the sands and take a dip in the water. To get to Peaks Island, take a water taxi

or the Casco Bay Lines Ferry out of Portland, and it's a quick ride across the bay to the island. Bringing your vehicle is frowned upon; exploring the island by bike or renting a golf cart is suggested. There are docks for private boats at the Peaks Island landing. The back shore section of Peaks affords stunning views of Casco Bay and some of its islands. It is a very slow pace

Opposite: Swiftly moving storms sweep across Casco Bay, churning up the sea and tossing underwater treasures onto the shore.

Left: Collecting sea glass along Sandy Beach in the shadow of spectacular sunsets on Peaks Island.

on the island, as the amusements of the early twentieth century are now gone. There are only two public restrooms on the island, so plan accordingly. During the height of summer, the island gets extremely busy; the charm of the island is best experienced in May and September.

CLIFF ISLAND, CASCO BAY

Cliff Island is a gorgeous island with approximately sixty-five year-round residents on the far eastern edge of Casco Bay. This very quiet island is accented by sweeping ledges that overlook the waters of the Atlantic Ocean. There used to be several inns for visitors during its heyday, like the Aucocisco House (which means "marshy place" in the Abenaki language), which advertised great views of Casco Bay and a "table abounding in good food."

Today, there are a variety of privately owned Victorian-era summer cottages that recall those days. There are no paved roads on the island, just dirt paths that lead from place to place. The 302-acre island is best explored on foot or via golf cart. One of the island's claims to fame is that it was the location of the movie *The Whales of August*, which was filmed in 1986 starring Bette Davis, Lillian Gish and Vincent Price.

A fascinating legend persists from the late 1700s about a hermit who lived on the island and was a reputed mooncusser. The origins of the term "mooncusser" are quite interesting. It is said that because the moon's rays mirror and enhance the water's surface, sailors could see very well on moonlit nights, even when the moon was only partially full. Therefore, decoy lanterns would not fool experienced mariners under these circumstances. As such, when the mooncusser's deceptions failed, he often shouted, "Cuss the moon!" into the moonlit night. Captain Keiff was thought to be a smuggler and a pirate, and he lived all alone on the island. During storms, Keiff would fasten a lantern to his horse's neck and ride back and forth across a narrow stretch of the island in hopes that he would lure passing vessels to their doom on the treacherous reefs. Ships that were hoping for shelter from the storms became wrecked on the island with no escape. Oftentimes the crew would fall victim to the combination of the perilous shoals and unrelenting weather.

The legend goes on to say that Captain Keiff would make sure that there were no survivors, and he would bury the bodies of the unfortunate sailors on a grassy knoll near a deep ravine. According to the story, it was called "Keiff's garden." Keiff would then salvage the ship's cargo and any valuables he could find, making for a unique way of life. After his mission was complete, he would return to his log hut to await the next storm.

Stinky Beach is located near the schoolhouse on Cliff Island and is a small rocky area that is fun to explore for sea glass. There are also two publicly accessible beaches near the ACE Ballfield. This protected shoreline is an ideal place to beachcomb, watch migrating birds and see the views across Casco Bay.

SORRENTO

A hidden gem of a town, Sorrento sits on Waukeag Neck, which used to be part of the town of Sullivan until 1895. Waukeag is a word used by the

Sorrento, Maine, is situated on a quiet peninsula overlooking Frenchman's Bay.

Penobscot and Maliseet Native tribes that describes the glacial formation that left a deposit of gravel and sand. The neck of land is surrounded by islands, two of which are nature preserves; it's not uncommon to see bald eagles in the area. The location, just four miles across Frenchman's Bay from Bar Harbor, was ideal as a summer resort for travelers. Daily train service to Boston brought more people to the growing community.

Sorrento saw a lot of growth in the late nineteenth century due to a man named Frank Jones from Portsmouth, New Hampshire. Frank was what you would call a Gilded Age robber baron, someone who was an especially shrewd and savvy capitalist. He owned the largest brewery in America, the Frank Jones Brewery, located in Portsmouth. In addition, he started water companies and owned several major factories, businesses and hotels. He was president of the Boston and Maine Railroad and served as a congressman. While he was serving in Washington, D.C., he met Delana B. Curtis, who became his mistress for nearly thirty years. He built a magnificent house called Rock End Cottage for Delana on West Cove, which still stands today. Frank also built the Hotel Sorrento in 1889, which boasted one hundred rooms, a fine dining restaurant, a billiard room and a bowling alley. A later addition added another fifty rooms. A quick-moving fire that started in the boiler room burned down the hotel on June 27, 1906.

Life in Sorrento quieted down throughout much of the twentieth century, and there are fewer than three hundred year-round residents in the town today. Sea glassing the area around the town dock and across from the town green yields abundant finds that may connect back to the hotel and some of the Victorian visitors to the island. The fragrant, woodsy balsam in the air adds an extra sensory element to the experience of beachcombing here.

CRANBERRY ISLES/ISLESFORD

The town of Cranberry Isles is made up of five islands just south of Mount Desert Island. Little Cranberry Island (also known as Islesford) is about a twenty-minute boat ride from Mount Desert Island. This small settlement of approximately two hundred summer residents and sixty-five year-round residents holds a community charm that speaks to a slower-paced life. The name "Cranberry Isles" comes from the native wild cranberries that were discovered on the islands. In 1791, Samuel Hadlock moved from Mount Desert Island to Little Cranberry, as he had acquired a large piece of property on the island. Six years prior, his father brought the family to the area from Ipswich, Massachusetts. There was a free-spirited desire by many to live unencumbered on a coastal Maine island. Samuel eventually opened a store in 1808 on the island and built many ships, some of which were commanded by his sons. Sadly, four of Samuel's five sons died or were lost at sea. In 1848, a few years before Samuel's death, the schooner the *Samuel Hadlock* was built on the island, and his only remaining son, Edwin, became the master.

When traveling to the island, you can take the tour boats from Northeast Harbor or the daily mailboat. On the approach to the island, a long, pebble-filled beach can be seen that goes under the Islesford Dock Restaurant and fishermen's co-op. The rustic restaurant with its weathered timbers is said to be the inspiration for the Krusty Krab, the undersea restaurant in the popular Nickelodeon series *Spongebob Squarepants*. Stephen Hillenburg, the creator of the series, was a marine biologist who spent some time on the island. There is even a story that a grumpy cook who worked there years ago was the inspiration for the Squidward Tentacles character.

Once you are done with lunch and collecting abundant bits of sea glass and pottery underneath the docks, a walk to the Congregational church is an absolute must. The church is home to the Ashley Bryan Center and pavilion. Ashley was born in Harlem, New York, to a West Indian family, and he was known for saying he was born with an artist's brush in his hand. He upcycled and re-created trash into incredible treasured artworks, puppets, paintings and sculptures. His studio was full of all sorts of discarded finds that he had a vision for. While he was a world traveler and teacher and even spent time in the service during World War II, he was at home on Little Cranberry Island. The illustrator of many books, he was inspired by Black poets, and he had a deeply spiritual side. His sincerity, articulate nature and humanitarian work made him an inspiration to those who met him.

Ashley collected sea glass from the island, and he used papier-mâché to hold the glass pieces together for his creations of mosaic stained-glass windows that can be found at the Congregational church. The windows tell the life story of Jesus Christ, and the way the glass pieces are shaped reflects the light through with an almost ethereal glow. Ashley passed away at the age of ninety-eight in February 2022, yet his special light still shines in many ways and especially through his beautifully crafted sea glass windows.

BAR HARBOR/GOULDSBORO

The area known as Mount Desert Island was explored by Samuel de Champlain in 1604. It was originally known as Eden in 1796, and its natural rugged beauty attracted famous artists and the wealthy throughout the nineteenth century. A devastating fire in 1947 that took nearly a month to fully extinguish burned over seventeen thousand acres of the island, including many of the summer homes.

Bar Island (which is technically located in Gouldsboro) was once known as Rodick Island, and there was a variety of buildings and a farm on the property. There was a busy canoe club out on the island, complete with a clubhouse in the late 1800s, and high society parties used to take place there. Documented stories of lavish tea parties, dancing and fancy suppers were told.

In 1909, the Rodick family house was moved off the island with the assistance of log rollers. A beautiful cottage known as the Bungalow stood on the south shore of the island from 1907 to 1943, when it burned to the ground. There are still ruins from the structure on the island, and part of the dock pilings still stick out of the water. In 2003, the National Park Service took over ownership of the island in full when it purchased twelve acres of land owned by NBC News correspondent Jack Perkins, who lived in a small home on the island called Moosewood. The home was removed in 2010, but there are remnants that can still be found along the island trails.

Walking out to Bar Island at low tide is quite an experience, and there is so much to see every step of the way. There are always crabs on the move, interesting shells, starfish and barnacles large and small amid a field of vibrant green seaweed. The sound of the tumbling rocks and pebbles in the tide is almost musical and meditative. The Bar Island Path land bridge is a half mile long, and the best accessible point is to take Bridge Street to the trail entrance. The natural land bridge here is accessible approximately two hours before low tide until two hours after low tide. There are numerous warning signs in the area to be mindful of the tides so you don't become stranded on the island.

The Shore Path trail on the eastern side of Bar Harbor, near the town pier, is another area worthy of exploration, as there are several places to walk out onto the rocky shore. The half-mile path dates to the 1880s and goes past many notable buildings and landmarks in town. Along this seaside trail you will find Balance Rock, which is a glacial erratic stone that was moved hundreds of miles by glacial ice. There are many historic photos of people posing with this seaside curiosity on the beach. The tide rises and falls up to eleven feet here twice each day, so if you decide to go down to the water, be sure to be aware of the tide times.

Mowry Beach, Lubec

Established around 1775, the town of Lubec sits at the entrance to Passamaquoddy Bay and was named for a town in Germany. Once part of Eastport, the naturally protected location made it the perfect place to establish a port. Lubec is also the gateway to the beautiful Canadian island of Campobello, where President Franklin Delano Roosevelt kept a summer home, which still can be visited. A trading post operated on nearby Treat's Island; however, smuggling was rampant in the early history of this border town. Fishermen knew how to navigate the isolated coves and islands where they could avoid the customs agents—and their fees. Goods from Britain were especially desirable and were exchanged for lumber and other natural resource products. During this time, the town flourished with several mills that worked with the strong tides. Fish processing and shipbuilding also brought prosperity, as did visitors and trade to the town.

When prohibition was spurred on because of the temperance movement that began in 1851, smuggling became even more of a problem. Local hotels were able to discreetly serve thirsty travelers rum, beer or other forms of alcohol that they could illegally obtain. In the January 15, 1883 edition of the *Portland Daily Press*, an article describes the circumstances around a smuggling case: "It seems like a melodrama to hear how on cold stormy nights in winter, when not a star could be seen, and in summer, when thick fogs and black darkness brooded over the sea, long boats, pulled their strong nervous arms, (the lookouts anxiously keeping watch for any suspicious lights.)"

"Booze dispensaries" were opened on nearby Campobello Island and attracted thirsty folk from Lubec to hop aboard the ferries and pay them a visit. These notorious "thirst shops" would make sure that their patrons were full of alcohol, along with any unusual container they carried with them across the border. Upon any questioning by authorities on the return trip to Lubec, those containers would be tossed overboard into the channel.

By 1890, the channel had become so busy with maritime trade and visiting steamships that the Lubec Channel Lighthouse was built to help aid navigation. The lighthouse, which is sometimes referred to as looking like a large spark plug, was automated in the 1960s. It still stands in the channel and is visible from the shores of Mowry Beach. The expansive beach was originally known as the Jabez Mowry "pasture lot." Jabez was a wealthy merchant who profited in part from the smuggling trade but left nearby Eastport, as investigations were underway into many questionable incidents that he was involved in. He built many important structures in Lubec, like the first church, the schoolhouse and the post office, among other places. The property eventually became part of a land trust and is now preserved by the Downeast Coastal Conservancy.

The beach entrance can be found at the end of Pleasant Street, and there is over a mile of beach to explore here. A colorful collection of migrating birds can be found, along with the remnants of a sunken forest that date to the ice age. The sweeping views are unforgettable, and when the tide is at its lowest, there is so much area to cover. Here you'll discover driftwood, brick bits, lots of pebbles and a perfect gritty sand to create smooth sea glass along the shore.

CHAPTER 5

NEW HAMPSHIRE

When seeking contentment, pleasure or recreation by New Hampshire's shore you'll find a pleasant revelation. In its ever changing landscape there's beauty and charm spread bounteously before us from nature's arms, where the restless ocean rolls on—in storm and peace, where verdant green meets sandy beach. Where the blue of heaven meets the sea. New Hampshire coast towns welcome thee. Nearing winding Piscataqua and its inland streams, by the homes of patriots and statesmen pause and dream. 'Neath stately elms, colonial mansions yet stand, rich in tradition and craftsmanship of a master hand.
—written on the back of a photo of an antique sea captain's home in the files of the Portsmouth Athenaeum

The Granite State of New Hampshire is home to the smallest coastline of any U.S. state, at just eighteen miles. While visitors to the state are generally attracted to the White Mountains for all the majestic beauty they offer in every season, from hiking to skiing, the seacoast is rich in colonial history and is home to one of the oldest cities in the country, Portsmouth, which was settled in 1623. The protected port of Portsmouth was vital in the New World as a major shipbuilding center, and countless merchant ships traveled up and down the tidal Piscataqua River. Fort William and Mary was built in 1632 at the mouth of the river to help protect the port and still stands today as Fort Constitution. Portsmouth was also the colonial capital of New Hampshire, and there are still a handful of beautifully maintained seventeenth-century homes in the city.

The *El Galeon* is a replica of a seventeenth-century ship that is docked for the tall ship festival along the Piscataqua River.

The coast extends from the town of Seabrook to the communities of Hampton and Rye before reaching Portsmouth. Throughout the summer, all these towns and their beaches become popular vacation destinations. The shore drive along Route 1B is one of the most scenic in New England, with several places to stop and explore the water's edge. There is no shortage of tidepools to glimpse, quiet coves and sweeping rock ledges that reach out into the sea like the ancient arms of mother earth. There is something special about beachcombing in New Hampshire, and you'll find yourself visiting this small coastal community of cities and towns repeatedly.

New Castle

There are so many towns in New Hampshire that are true hidden gems, and the village of New Castle has a colonial charm, with many houses that date back to the 1600s. New Castle was once part of nearby Portsmouth and is sometimes still referred to as the "Great Island." It is accessible from the causeway leading out of Portsmouth's south end or across the bridge at Little Harbor adjacent from the Wentworth by the Sea hotel. The island is just one square mile and is situated at the mouth of the Piscataqua River, which leads into the port of Portsmouth.

Originally settled as a fishing village on the river in the seventeenth century, New Castle's strategic location made it an ideal location for military fortifications over the years. The Great Island Common is a thirty-two-acre park and beach that is tucked behind the town library. An active military post called Camp Langdon—named for Governor John Langdon, who was a Revolutionary War hero—used to stand on the site. The installation had several buildings, including a hospital and armory, which occupied the area until the 1960s, when it was converted into a park.

The maritime traffic that has traveled past the park over four hundred years of the colonial settlement is intriguing in so many ways. Fishing, lumbering and trading were some of the early industries that were established, which eventually expanded to privateering and shipbuilding. Some of the fastest ships in the world, known as clippers, came out of this port. In fact, the importance of the port is reflected in the lighthouse that stands just beyond the edge of the beach at the Great Island Common. Portsmouth Harbor Lighthouse was the first lighthouse established north of Boston, in 1771, and originally it stood within the walls of Fort William and Mary, which is visible from the waterfront. The current tower, made of cast-iron panels, was built in 1878 and stands at the edge of a walkway extending from the fort wall. The first federal shipyard in the United States was established just up the river a short way from the lighthouse in 1800.

On the opposite shore from the beach at the common is Fort Foster at Kittery Point. Originally, that was the site of the four-story, two-hundred-room Pocahontas Hotel, which was displaced for the establishment of the fort when it opened in the late 1800s. After World War II, the fort eventually reverted to the Town of Kittery and can be visited for a nominal fee. There is a legend of a mysterious ghostly woman in a red dress who is seen walking the beach at the fort around sunset.

Above: The tall ship *Lynx* sails by the Great Island Common in New Castle, New Hampshire.

Left: The treasure from an afternoon of sea glass searching in New Castle, New Hampshire.

The stone tower of Whaleback lighthouse can be seen just offshore from the beach at Fort Foster. The lighthouse was established due to countless shipwrecks that happened on the stone ledge, which is obscured at high tide. There are accounts of ocean waves overtaking the fifty-nine-foot tower during storms and breaking the glass windows, and several lighthouse keepers even died while living and working in the lighthouse. You can also catch a glimpse of the recently restored Wood Island Life Saving Station, which dates to 1908. For forty years, surfmen, as they were known, shoved off in wooden rowboats to aid floundering vessels, no matter how heavy the seas.

The beach at the Great Island Common is surrounded by so many historic tales that it is easy to float back through the pages of time to imagine it. John Paul Jones's famous ship the USS *Ranger* was launched nearby in 1777 bound for Paris, France. In the nineteenth century, Portsmouth was home to some of the largest breweries in America, which shipped out all over the Northeast via rail and boat. Over seventy-five submarines were built at the Portsmouth Naval Shipyard in the twentieth century. The possibilities of what you can find on the beach here are endless, with active maritime traffic passing by on a regular basis. There is a fee to use the park in season; however, there are lots of picnic areas and a restroom as well. The views are just breathtaking for the beachcomber, from old forts to lighthouses and even a distant view of the Isles of Shoals off on the easterly horizon.

There have been several ghostly sightings along the shore here. Reports of a spirit that wears a lighthouse keeper's uniform have been shared by numerous visitors and some members of the Coast Guard over the years. Many folks believe the spirit to be that of Joshua Card, who proudly kept the light at Portsmouth Harbor for thirty-five years and was forced into retirement at the age of eighty-six. Perhaps Joshua is still tending to his duties and keeping a keen watch over this old, storied seaport.

STAR ISLAND

Every year the popularity of the Shoals is greater than it was the year before. The islands have a charm that is difficult to explain.
—New York Daily Tribune, *October 8, 1874*

About seven miles off the New Hampshire coast are nine rocky islands with a rugged scenic beauty known as the Isles of Shoals. Steeped in legends and lore, the islands are a mysterious place with a fascinating history that makes explorations especially intriguing. Ongoing archaeological excavations indicate that the Native American people were present on the islands at least six thousand years ago. The isles were also a waystation for pirates and their scurvy mates, and in the seventeenth century, the location was a prosperous fishing station boasting two taverns and a meetinghouse. Reportedly, Black Sam Bellamy of the *Whydah* stopped there for supplies. Spanish ships with their hulls full of New World cargo stopped at the Isles of Shoals to load up with salted cod before making the long voyage back to Spain. Many of these galleons are believed to have sunk near the islands, leaving their rich cargoes underwater. A man named William Babb, who was Captain Kidd's first mate, settled there. According to legend, his ghost is still seen wandering the islands with the scar of a hangman's noose around his neck.

Another long-told ghost story on the isles is about the spirit of a woman who has been seen dressed in a long coat and stands on an outcropping of rock saying, "He will return." She is believed to be the companion of the infamous pirate Blackbeard, who was rumored to visit the island and bury some riches there. The ghostly woman is believed to stand guard over the treasure until his return.

Five of the islands are officially charted as Maine, including the largest island, called Appledore, which was a thriving arts community in the nineteenth century and was frequented by Nathaniel Hawthorne and John Greenleaf Whittier, among other luminaries of that time. Nearby Smuttynose Island is famous for the double axe murder that took place there in 1873, which inspired both the book and the movie *The Weight of Water* by Anita Shreve. Did a man named Louis Wagner commit the heinous crime, or was it the one surviving woman who lived to tell the tale? Based on witness testimony and circumstantial evidence, Louis was executed in 1875 by hanging for the murder of Karen Christensen and Anethe Christensen; however, there are many theories about other suspects that are still being investigated today.

A church constructed from the timbers of a wrecked Spanish ship in 1685 was established on Star Island, which later became the town of Gosport. While that church saw a fire in 1790, the current structure was built in 1800. There was a tradition of islanders carrying lanterns to church services in long processionals up the hill. It is believed that on certain nights, you can still see the long line of ghostly flickering candle lights along the pathways.

While Star Island was home to many colorful fishermen (according to a nineteenth-century report, a certain fisherman on Star Island was known to

Star Island, off the coast of New Hampshire, remains largely unchanged since the nineteenth century and is an ideal place to discover sea-worn treasures.

polish off four gallons of rum in a single month), the location was thought to be the perfect place to build a grand resort hotel in 1873. The Oceanic Hotel had a dining room that could seat four hundred people along with a billiard room, bar, grocery and options for a warm or cool saltwater or freshwater bath. Sadly, after three seasons, the original Oceanic burned to the ground. The fire was so intense that the glow of the flames was said to be visible from Boston. Before the ashes of the first building had cooled, a new Oceanic Hotel was built. In 1915, the Star Island Corporation purchased the island and the buildings there for a religious retreat center. Guests are still welcomed at the Oceanic, and it is like traveling back in time. The rooms are quite simplistic; most doors do not have locks, and there are no phones or televisions in the rooms either. A rustic, community camp feel is what greets visitors, along with the bell ringing for assembly for community-style meals. A section of the upper floor of the hotel is known as "Ghost Alley" because of the reports of people hearing calliope music and phantom footsteps and experiencing spirited sightings. There are also two nineteenth-century cemeteries on the island worth checking out during a visit.

A large collection of sea glass is assembled on the rocky shore of Star Island.

A peaceful exploration of Star and Smuttynose Islands is an unforgettable experience. When it comes to looking for sea treasures, it is not uncommon to find little artistic collages and piles of sea glass or surf-tumbled pottery along the pathways and nature trails. Sea glass is sometimes left by island visitors as a token at the altar in the Gosport church. The small pebble-filled beaches are perfect for sifting through while watching the boats come and go

Beachcombing on Star Island yields a variety of finds like dishware, old porcelain pipe stems, melted (bonfire) glass and interesting pottery bits.

to the island. Each piece can tell a little history of the island, whether from its piracy days or the era when it was an oceanside Victorian retreat.

Private boats are welcome in Gosport Harbor, or you can book a ticket on the Isles of Shoals Steamship aboard the M/V *Thomas Leighton* or via the Island Cruises Company aboard the *Uncle Oscar*. Be sure to wear comfortable shoes, dress in layers and pack some snacks for your visit, as there are very limited resources on the island.

ODIORNE STATE PARK, RYE

Spend some time exploring the many rocky beaches of Rye along Ocean Boulevard, and be sure to include a visit to Odiorne State Park along Route 1A near the Seacoast Science Center. The location was the first European settlement in what was to become New Hampshire. The oceanfront park is also the former site of Fort Dearborn during World War II, and the property became a state park in 1961. There are some wonderful cellar holes, tidepools and stony beachfront to explore here. In addition, there are three hundred acres of parkland here with nature trails and a scenic picnic area, making it an ideal location for a day trip. There is a small fee to use the park in the season, and there is a separate fee to visit the Science Center.

CHAPTER 6
MASSACHUSETTS

My life is like a stroll upon the beach,
As near the ocean's edge as I can go;
My tardy steps its waves sometimes o'erreach,
Sometimes I stay to let them overflow.

My sole employment is, and scrupulous care,
To place my gains beyond the reach of tides,—
Each smoother pebble, and each shell more rare,
Which Ocean kindly to my hand confides.
—excerpt from "The Fisher's Boy," Henry David Thoreau

With over two hundred miles of coastline, the Bay State offers a variety of experiences for the beachcomber, from busy beaches around Boston Harbor to the serenity of the far reaches of the dunes of Cape Cod. The beaches in Massachusetts welcomed the explorers and settlers of the New World back in the seventeenth century, and there are echoes of that history rooted in many of these sites. Boston Harbor and the Massachusetts Bay have legendary ties to famous battles and colonial unrest. The sheltered harbors helped the colony grow rapidly through maritime trade with ports from around the globe.

Devastating storms and historic weather events in Massachusetts are still talked about across the generations. Many of the beaches are still being shaped by the blizzards, nor'easters and floods, which makes explorations here particularly fascinating. Winds and waves have washed entire sections of the sea floor across the shores of Massachusetts. The *Boston Daily Globe* reported after a severe storm in November 1888:

Nantasket Beach Lined With Wrecks
Off Scituate Fifteen Mariners Drowned
Many Schooners Swallowed by the Sea

Old Ocean ruled supreme yesterday. From Old Newbury to Provincetown the power of the mad sea waves was acknowledged by every man who knew what the ocean was when it was "real mad." The shore was bombarded and assailed by the most furious storm that New England has seen for the past—well, some say 10 and some say 35 years.

It was a big storm at any rate, and the residents of the north shore, from Marblehead to Boston, can attest to its violence. Seeking news and wishing to get the latest information regarding the triumphs of the storm, a Globe artist took a flying trip to Point Shirley and Ocean Spray yesterday afternoon and saw the ravages of the elements. It was a grand spectacle. From the famous hostelry of Tafts on Point Shirley away up on the bluff of Great Head and the beach from Shirley Station to Ocean Spray, and away up on the Winthrop Highlands, the shore was covered with debris, cast up by the "sad sea waves" in their eagerness to capture still more of terra-firma and encroach upon the domains of land.

At Great Head the scene was perhaps commonplace. Lobster pots lay in the front yards of cottages, men went along the streets picking up lobsters and crabs from the sidewalks and garden areas and seaweed clung to the fences for rods and rods.

Beachcombers will find that their visits to the coastline here will be quite historic as they follow in the footsteps of those who helped shape the history of America. In this chapter, you will discover a variety of reasons and historic events as to why Massachusetts is a perfect destination for sea glass collecting. What sort of adventure would you like to take, and what will you find here? Let's find that perfect mix of surf, sand, history and sea glass.

BOURNE

The gateway to Cape Cod, Bourne is made up of ten different villages, including Buzzards Bay, Sagamore, Pocasset and Gray Gables. Originally a Pilgrim and Native American trading post in the early 1600s, the area was settled as part of the Town of Sandwich by 1640 before finally being incorporated as the Town of Bourne in 1884. Gray Gables was the site of the first summer White House on the Cape, built in 1880 as the summer home of Grover Cleveland while he was the mayor of Buffalo, New York. In later years, it served as his summer White House when he was president. He received his second nomination as the Democratic presidential candidate from special telegraph wires installed in Gray Gables by the *Boston Globe* and the Associated Press. The massive house boasted twelve fireplaces and a dock to accommodate a navy gunboat that was used by the first family. It was a six-mile carriage ride out to the sprawling estate.

In an 1892 published letter to the editor of the *Boston Globe*, Grover Cleveland wrote of his summer home: "I like my residence too, because my neighbors are of that independent sort who are not obtrusively curious.

A large piece of floral tile from the beach adjacent to President Grover Cleveland's summer home.

These beautiful pieces of porcelain and dishware came from the beach adjacent to President Grover Cleveland's summer house.

I have but to behave myself and pay my taxes to be treated like any other citizen of the United States." President Cleveland preferred an eclectic style to his collection of serving ware, as he chose to vary the design and coloring of the china for each course served.

The house was sold in the 1920s and was eventually converted to an inn and restaurant, which burned down in a spectacular fire on December 11, 1973. It took four fire departments to control the blaze, which started in a cobblestone fireplace that faced the Cape Cod Canal. Today, another gabled house stands on the site, but the house and property are privately owned.

The Gray Gables beach is on Gilder Road, and the geology there is a mix of marsh, sand and shallow water. With the beach being on the Cape Cod Canal, there is a lot of seafaring traffic and commercial ships to observe going by. Parking is very limited, as the beach is in a small neighborhood. Off-season exploration and beachcombing are encouraged. Pieces of porcelain, dinnerware and small artifacts of household items have washed ashore here over the years. (The original train station building for President Cleveland still exists at the Aptucxet Museum in town at 6 Aptucxet Road.)

Provincetown

*That blue water, so quiet now, and breaking with such gentle ripples on the
shore, does not give you the impression, that in a few hours with a change
of wind, it could be lashed into fury, and with towering foam capped waves
dash upon the beach with the roar of a Niagara.*

The storm is o'er, and all along the sandy reach,
The shining wavelets ripple on the lonely beach,
Beneath the storm washed sands and waves of blue,
There rests unclaimed, the members of the lost ship's crew.
  —Shipwrecks on Cape Cod *(Hyannis, MA: Goss Printers, 1920)*

In Provincetown, located at the very end of Cape Cod, the natural beauty
and the miles of untouched landscape beckon visitors to spend their
days exploring all this vibrant seaside town has to offer. The *Mayflower*
made landfall at Provincetown on November 21, 1620, and while there,
the passengers wrote the Mayflower Compact, declaring themselves a
democratic commonwealth. The Pilgrim monument, which was completed
in 1910, is in the center of town and pays tribute to that event. Three miles
long and two streets wide, the town is surrounded on three sides by water.
Provincetown remained a small community during the Revolutionary days;
in 1800, there were 812 people who lived there, but by 1855, the population
had more than tripled to 3,096. Portuguese sailors also came over to make
their fortune in the rich fishing waters. Ships had to navigate around the
tip of Provincetown until the Cape Cod Canal was completed in 1914.
By the early 1900s, the beaches were crowded by rows of artists, and the
town has been referred to as the oldest continuous art colony in America.
Many artists who have created works there have said that the natural light in
Provincetown is like nowhere else in the world.

Some of the shipwrecks here are legendary, with the HMS *Somerset III*
being one of the most intriguing. The ship, which had terrorized other
vessels along the coast during the American Revolution, was wrecked on
November 2, 1778, while pursuing a French ship. It hit the Peaked Hill Bars,
a sandbar sometimes still referred to as Dead Man's Hollow. Many people
in town stood on the hill and watched the dramatic events unfold. Of the
crew, 21 men perished in the wreck, and the captain was forced to walk to
Provincetown to be exchanged for two American officers. The rest of the
crew, reported to be 480 in number, were taken prisoner by the locals and

It is not unusual to find fully intact antique bottles along the beaches of Provincetown, Massachusetts.

then marched to Boston. The remnants of the wreck are still embedded in the sandbar, and it has been exposed three times in 1886, 1973 and 2016. In December 1902, a pistol thought to be from the ship washed ashore, and in June 1917, a musket washed ashore that was made in 1776 and was also rumored to come from the wreck.

The *Annie Spindler* ran aground off Race Point in 1922 carrying six hundred cases of Canadian whiskey. The crew had tied themselves to the ship's rigging as they tried to ride out the freezing cold storm bearing down on them. The men were rescued, but there was the matter of the goods that they were carrying during Prohibition times. The paperwork the ship was carrying said that they were bound for the West Indies, but that was typical of the rumrunners of the day. It was speculated that they were on the way to Plymouth. The Coast Guard removed the cargo and stored it in a warehouse while the determination was made of what to do next. According to legend, despite the rough waters, it was said that brave folks dove into the waves to see if they could find any whiskey. The *Fall River Daily News* reported that scores of people from all over the Cape swarmed into town with the "prospect of having some of the 600 cases of whiskey come washing ashore." Eventually, another ship was summoned to pick up the cargo; it, too, had papers to take the goods to the West Indies. It was no surprise to many that the ship soon ended up in Plymouth. The *Annie Spindler* eventually became a weather-worn wreck that became a bit of a playground for the local children.

The September 1, 1926 edition of the *Boston Globe* reported the following:

Stranded Rum Runner on Point Race Beach Now "Play Boat" For Campers' Children. High up on the shelving beach at Race Point on the bend of Cape Cod which faces the sweep of the Atlantic Ocean, lies the rum-runner Annie Spindler—*a stout schooner, built at Lunenburg, Nova Scotia—now a play house and picture resort for the children of Summer Campers. Children have made swings of the riggings and the cabin, with bunks where captain and officers slept, is now the play room and dining room of laughing boys and girls from all over the country.*

One of the most tragic shipwrecks in the history of New England, the paddle wheel steamship *Portland* sank on its voyage from Boston to Maine in what became known as the Portland Gale of 1898. One of the most devastating storms, it sank 187 vessels and claimed the lives of 456 people around the region on November 26 and 27, 1898. The passengers were heading back home after Thanksgiving celebrations. The wreck of the steamer *Portland* became known as the *Titanic* of New England. All 130 passengers and more than 60 crew members perished. It wasn't until 1989 that the *Portland* was located, but it took until 2002 to confirm it. Located off Cape Ann, the wreck is 460 feet down on Stellwagen Bank, New England's only marine sanctuary. It has been theorized that when the storm was at its height, the captain tried to bring the ship into the harbor at Provincetown, due to some reports that were given during the storm. After the storm passed, 38 bodies washed ashore on Cape Cod beaches. Debris from the *Portland*, including a life preserver, was recovered at Race Point station as the high tide receded. A curious book in the collection of the Provincetown Historical Society is connected to the disaster. Published in 1895, it is a hardcover edition of a book of poems by Edgar Allan Poe. Penciled in the cover it reads: "This book was washed ashore from the steamer Portland in 1898...Donald B. MacMillan."

The current lighthouse at Long Point was built in 1873 and marks the entrance to Provincetown Harbor. It was an ideal location for a fishing village, which sprang up out there in the early nineteenth century. There

The amazing sea glass windows crafted by Ashley Bryant can be seen in the Congregational church on Islesford.

Left: Beautiful blue and aqua sea glass that comes from old glass insulators and canning jars on the beaches of Jamestown, Rhode Island.

Below: A swirly rainbow piece of antique Sandwich Glass pulled out of the salt marsh that was adjacent to the original factory.

Above: The door of the brick oil house next to Portsmouth Harbor Lighthouse was washed away in a storm after a recent restoration.

Left: The old lighthouses of Cape Cod like the Nobska Light in Woods Hole remind visitors how challenging it was for mariners to navigate the sometimes treacherous coastline.

Left: Motif Number 1 in Rockport harbor is an iconic symbol of the settlement; the original 1840 structure was destroyed in the Blizzard of 1978, but a replica was rebuilt later that year.

Below: Within this assortment of bottle tops is a curved piece of frosted green glass, sometimes referred to as a "sea pickle."

Right: Blue-striped yellow-ware bowl fragments from the 1930s that have been discovered on Deer Island recall the almshouse and prison that used to stand there.

Below: Blue willow patterned porcelain and chinaware was extremely popular in the late eighteenth and nineteenth centuries.

Top: There are so many shades of green sea glass. The color green is made out of iron, copper or chromium.

Middle: Pirate glass looks black, but when placed in the light, its true color can be seen, which can vary from brown to purple and green.

Bottom: Decorative green dishware reveals edge and bottom shapes that help identify the type of vessel it originally was.

Left: There are so many ways to connect with maritime history in Newport, Rhode Island; sea glass collecting is just one of them.

Below: The pediment of this house in Newport, Rhode Island, is full of large pieces of well-worn sea glass.

Left: Several years of
sea glass collecting on
Corporation Beach in Dennis,
Massachusetts, yielded a
variety of pastels in a variety
of textures and grades.

Below: A mix of different types
of glass vessels in a window is
perfect for displaying sea glass.

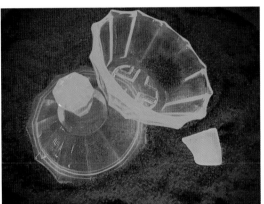

Top: A sunset orange piece of carnival glass is a rare find. While it's not entirely frosted, it was too nice to pass up during one beachcombing adventure.

Middle: Uranium glass dates from the mid-nineteenth century to the mid-twentieth century and is highly prized by collectors.

Bottom: A colorful collection of nineteenth-century paperweights on display at the Sandwich Glass Museum.

Left: Countless wharves framed Boston Harbor, and green glass is easily spotted among the broken industrial remnants and bricks along the shoreline.

Below: Two of the most commonly found colors of clear and brown glass along with white porcelain and pottery fragments are abundant throughout the shorelines of Boston Harbor.

Above: Beautiful antique blue bottles found by Dick Scott under the waves of New Hampshire waters.

Left: Cobalt blue sea glass is a favorite among sea glass collectors and was originally used in the nineteenth century for medicine and poison bottles.

Above: Colorful pieces of dishware and pottery look great displayed in clear glass containers surrounded by vintage postcards of the beach or location where the treasure was found.

Left: Old printer's trays are a great way to display and showcase your sea glass and beach-found treasures.

Right: Weather conditions on Cape Cod are oftentimes fast changing, and a clear, sunny day at the beach can very quickly turn into a moody, foggy day along the shore.

Below: Pink glass, called Depression glass, was manufactured in the 1920s and 1930s. It was an affordable, mass-produced form of molded glassware.

Left: Scituate
Lighthouse is an
important guiding
light over the town's
busy harbor and
has withstood many
devastating storms.

Below: Colorful
collections are
gathered piece by
piece over many
years with patience
and a keen eye.

A frosted brown glass ring handle to an old jug bottle.

Frosting or sugaring of sea glass happens when the stone and sand etches and pits the surface of the glass.

Top: Bonfire glass often holds fragments of ash, wood, metal and sand that adhered to the melted glass.

Middle: The manufacture of glass mason jars began in the 1850s, and jar shards are commonly found all over New England beaches.

Bottom: Glass insulators were manufactured from the 1840s to the 1960s and were used for telegraph and telephone lines to keep them from grounding out.

were six windmills, a post office, a general store and two hundred people who lived there. After about fifty years, due to the remoteness of the location and declining fishing numbers, most of the people in the village decided to pack up and leave. Between thirty and forty families who left took their houses with them and floated them across the harbor back to the town. Today, these "Long Point Floaters" can be found in town, and they are marked with white and blue plaques showing a floating house in the water.

The residents of Provincetown during the age of sail were quite thrifty and salvaged what they could from shipwrecks; house timbers and fence posts were made from ships' masts, and old ships' sails were used for rugs. Clammers who dredge Provincetown Harbor continue to pull up all sorts of interesting items like anchors, muskets, whale bones and, of course, old bottles. There were also over fifty wharves that reached out in the harbor at one time. In the 1950s and 1960s, local youths would jump off the wharves to catch coins that were thrown in the water by ferryboat passengers.

Pamet Harbor in Truro, Massachusetts, offers well-weathered sea glass in small quantities.

There are several great places to find sea glass in Provincetown, including Race Point Beach and Long Point (which is a two-and-a-half-mile walk). Herring Cove is one of the best choices because the geology there offers the perfect stony, gritty sand for well-sugared sea glass. You want to be sure that you wear sturdy footwear to walk this beach. A long-handled scoop to sift through the tumbling stones in the surf can yield some treasures that may not have washed ashore just yet. When you're done with all your hard work, you can enjoy the spectacular sunsets from this west-facing beach.

Marblehead

At the beginning of the seventeenth century, Marblehead was a fishing station, serving as an outpost for fishermen who did not settle there. Gradually, families began to arrive, and Marblehead was established as a village in 1629. Many of the first settlers of the town came from Devon, Dorset and Cornwall, as well as the Channel Islands. The fish were reported to be so large and the harbor so full of them that a person could walk from one side of the harbor to the other on the backs of them without ever getting his feet wet. Marblehead is a small peninsula with a large, deep harbor with sheltering offshore islands, and it was part of nearby Salem for a time until it officially separated in 1649.

Throughout the eighteenth century, the wharves in Marblehead were quite busy, and trading vessels were constantly moving in and out of the harbor on the tide. It was recorded that eighty schooners sailed from the harbor and six hundred men and boys were employed in the seafaring industry, which was nearly the entire male population of the town. Boys as young as nine years old assisted the fishermen's work when they went out to the Grand Banks and were taught how to fish to support their families. In 1773, the schooner the *King's Boat* wrecked coming back from Baker Island in Salem. As the schooner approached Marblehead Harbor, it was taken by wind and wave. Ten lives were lost, and five of them were pregnant women. One couple was reported to be seen locked arm in arm as they sank beneath the waves. It has been told that they are said to remain in the same embrace on the ocean floor.

During the War of 1812, there were many Marblehead privateers who received letters of marque from President James Madison. Many of those on privateering ships were motivated to capture vessels (sometimes referred

One of the most sweeping views of Marblehead Harbor is from the top of Burial Hill.

to as "prizes") and bring them back, where the goods on the ship would be shared by the ship owners and crew. Many of the sailors were fishermen merchant mariners who were affected by the trade restrictions, blockades and embargo acts from Great Britain.

On April 3, 1814, the USS *Constitution* avoided a blockade in Boston Harbor and was being pursued by two British ships toward Cape Ann. Initially, the *Constitution* was going to head to Portsmouth, New Hampshire, but the wind was not favorable enough, so it headed south. To gain speed against the British, the crew of the *Constitution* dumped much of their supplies overboard, including water barrels and 1,500 gallons of rum. It was recorded in the local newspapers that people on shore gathered to see the spectacle as the *Constitution* pulled ahead and eventually made its way into Marblehead Harbor, where it dropped anchor. The British ships waited six miles offshore and didn't dare enter the harbor for fear that the guns at Fort Sewall might prove to be too challenging. Finally, the British were scared off when reports came from an ominous message that was relayed from Boston that the British would have to defend themselves against "a force from 10 to 12,000 men with a considerable train of artillery would have been in

Marblehead, to defend their favorite Constitution." After about ten days, the British sailed off, and the *Constitution* sailed on to nearby Salem Harbor.

There are many ghost stories along the beaches that echo across Marblehead Harbor, with some that date all the way back to the seventeenth century. There are stories about a man known as Wizard Dimond, who would be hired by ships' captains to enchant the weather for favorable conditions at sea. He would climb to the top of Old Burial Hill, which overlooks the harbor, and shout his commands to the weather while weaving between the gravestones. It is said that on quiet nights, his booming voice can still be heard echoing across the harbor.

An excerpt from *The History and Traditions of Marblehead*, published in 1880, speaks of the haunted waters around Marblehead:

> Stories of phantom ships seen at sea before the loss of a vessel; of the appearance on the water of loved ones who had died at home; footsteps and voices heard mysteriously in the still hours of the night coming as warnings from another world. Signs and omens which foretold the approaching death of some member of a family, or prophecies whispered by the wind that those away on the mighty deep would find a watery grave.
>
> These, and other stories of pirates met on the seas and smugglers who secreted their treasures along the shore, formed the burden of conversation through the long winter evenings. Of the many traditions of this nature, told with simple faith and sincere belief by our ancestors, few have come down to their descendants, and of these the story of the Screeching Woman is perhaps the most distinctly remembered.
>
> It was said that during the latter part of the seventeenth century a Spanish ship laden with rich merchandise was captured by pirates and brought into the harbor of Marblehead. The crew and every person on board the ill-fated ship had been murdered at the time of the capture, except a beautiful English lady, who the ruffians brought on shore near what is now called Oakum Bay, and there barbarously murdered her. The few fishermen who inhabited the place were absent, and the women and children who remained could do nothing to prevent the crime. The screams of the victim were loud and dreadful, and her cries of "Lord save me! Mercy! Oh! Lord Jesus, save me!" were distinctly heard. The body was buried where the crime was perpetrated, and for over one hundred and fifty years on the anniversary of that dreadful tragedy the screams of the poor woman were repeated in a voice so shrill and supernatural as to send an indescribable thrill of horror through all who heard them.

Throughout Marblehead are narrow, twisting streets that evolved from old cow paths throughout the village. Some people joke that there isn't a street that is in a straight line; however, all roads eventually lead to the shore and the beautiful harbor. The charm of this small town is found in every hillside overlooking the water. It's a terrific town to discover on foot, and around every corner is another piece of history to discover. Abbot Hall stands on a high point in the town and can be seen from the beach. Built in 1876, it is the current town hall. It contains a maritime museum and gift shop and houses the original *Spirit of '76* painting.

A defensive fort was established on Gale's Head in 1644. It was later enlarged and renamed Fort Sewall, and today it is a scenic waterfront park and a great place for a picnic over the harbor. Front Street leads to Fort Beach, the perfect place to explore the rocky beach and colorful tidepools for sea glass. The screaming woman beach is also located on Front Street next to the Barnacle restaurant. This is a perfect place to pick up pottery shards or old artifacts. A small, hidden beach that is in one of the oldest sections of town is Gas House Beach, which was named for the gas generating plant that stood on site to create gas for the town's street and house lamps. If the tide is low, you can walk over to Gerry's Island for more great beachcombing. Be mindful of the poison ivy that grows there and pay attention to the tide so that you don't become stranded.

Devereux Beach is five acres long and follows the causeway that leads out to Marblehead Neck. It is a great spot to comb for sea glass that has washed over from Boston Harbor. Chandler Hovey Park, at the end of the neck, is home to Marblehead Lighthouse, which was built in 1895. During the Hurricane of 1938, lighthouse keeper Marden kept the light in the tower going when the power went out by hooking it up to the battery in his car. While the storm did a lot of damage, the lighthouse in Marblehead burned brightly. This park is the perfect place to catch the sunset and set up your beachcombing finds and take photos with the town skyline and harbor as the perfect backdrop.

ROCKPORT

Rockport was originally called Sandy Bay and was a largely uninhabited part of Gloucester until the late 1600s, when land grants and property purchases were made. Small houses and log cabins were built in the early

1700s. In 1743, a dock was built on Sandy Bay for shipping timber and fishing. At that time, there were sixty-five houses and five hundred people living in Rockport. Four fishing schooners that made regular trips to the Grand Banks and twenty fishing vessels called the town their home port. In the 1800s, the first granite from Rockport quarries was shipped to cities and towns throughout the East Coast of the United States, adding more activity to the harbor.

It might be hard to believe that a town that banned alcohol for 162 years has some of the most colorful and abundant sea glass. Hannah Jumper, Rockport's legendary resident, was an herbalist and seamstress who led a movement to ban alcohol in the town. Reportedly, Hannah and two hundred hatchet-wielding women moved through the streets of town in 1856 hacking every barrel and bottle of liquor that they could find. According to the story, within a five-hour period, these women raided thirteen establishments and destroyed fifty barrels of alcohol, and they became known as the "Hatchet Gang." In a town where fishing was one of the largest industries, the legend was that rum was as important as bait for the fishermen.

Hannah was seventy-five years old while the temperance movement was going strong and was intent on ridding the community of demon alcohol, as sales had been rapidly climbing in recent years. A July 4 celebration had turned into a drunken mob scene, and it was then that Hannah and her gang calculated their next move. They had been secretly meeting behind closed doors at sewing circles and card parties, planning their rebellion. On July 8, the group assembled at the town pump at Dock Square, and the raid began at 9:00 a.m. There was such a commotion in the town that people likened the event to a parade, as everyone eagerly watched to see what happened next. One legendary incident happened during the raid at the Mount Pleasant House in town. The gang entered the house, believing that there was alcohol being hidden there. The woman of the house was sitting there rocking a cradle and told the group to stay away because the baby had smallpox. The women weren't afraid and couldn't be stopped, and when they pulled the blanket in the cradle back, there was a jug of whiskey that ended up meeting its fate with the blade of an axe. Rockport Harbor was said to be a giant punchbowl, and the smell of rum was like a cloud over the town. After the raids, it was made official that Rockport was going to proceed as a "dry" town, and the sale of alcohol was banned. The Sandy Bay Historical Society in Rockport has one of the banners carried in the raid as well as one of the axes that was used by one of the women.

Rockport eased the rules around alcohol consumption in restaurants in 2006, after more than a century of being one of the few dry communities in Massachusetts. Despite all the years of being a dry town, this is still a terrific place to find sea glass in several areas. You might catch divers over at Cape Hedge Beach, which is located at the end of Seaview Street, just beyond Pebble Beach. Parking here is scarce, as this is more of a secluded beach hidden behind an intricate stone wall; a bike ride is recommended. A wooden ramp that goes from the residents-only parking area will lead you to the beach. The stones here are tumbled smooth and round, and the terrain is vigorously tossed around on a regular basis. This is a great spot for bird-watching, and the views of Thacher Island are terrific. There are no amenities here, and it is best explored at low tide. Be sure to look between the stony sections as well for tumbled glass pieces that may have been launched up from the waves.

Front Street beach is located on Beach Street right around the corner from the restaurants, shops and art galleries and is a must visit. There are some metered spaces here, or there are lots where you can pay for parking in season. When the tide is high, most of the beach is submerged; however,

Front Beach in Rockport, Massachusetts, is a favorite of sea glass collectors, but it is quite busy in the summer season.

the waves leave behind lots of treasures when it goes back out. There are lots of ever-changing tidepools and pockets to explore. Be sure to canvass the entire beach, as sea glass can be found along the edges of the beach as well. There is a bathhouse that is open there in season when it tends to be much busier.

Rockport was hit by the Great Colonial Hurricane of 1635, which left a trail of destruction on Cape Ann and caused the wreck of the bark the *Watch and Wait* on what is now known as Thacher Island. The August storm tore at the sails of the ship, which was headed to Marblehead with twenty-three passengers. The captain dropped anchor as they tried to ride out the storm. At the height of the storm, the anchor was dragged and snapped off. There were only two survivors. Antony Thatcher and his wife survived by miraculously swimming to the island. He later described the incident:

We were by the violence of the waves and fury of the winds (by the Lord's permission) lifted upon a rock between two high rocks, yet all was one rock, but it raged with the stroke which came into the pinnace, so as we were presently up to our middle in water as we sat. The waves came furiously and violently over us, and against us; but by reason of the rock's proportion could not lift us off but beat her all to pieces. Now look with me upon our distress, and consider of my misery, who beheld the ship broken, the water in her, and violently overwhelming us, my goods and provisions swimming in the seas, my friends almost drowned, and mine own poor children so untimely (if I may so term it without offense), before my eyes drowned, and ready to be swallowed up, and dashed to pieces against the rocks by the merciless waves, and did myself ready to accompany them.

Once they found themselves on the island, Antony came to the grim realization that he and his wife were the only survivors of the shipwreck. They did their best to salvage what they could to survive. He wrote:

I and my wife were almost naked, both of us, and wet and cold even unto death. I found a knapsack cast upon the shore, in which I had a steel and flint and powder horn; going further I found a drowned goat; then I found a hat and my son William's coat, both of which I put on. My wife found one of her petticoats, which she put on. I found also two cheeses and some butter driven ashore. Thus the Lord sent us some clothes to put on and food to sustain our new lives which we had lately given unto us, and means also to make a fire, for in a horn I had some gunpowder which, to my own and since to other men's admiration, was dry. So taking a piece of my wife's neckcloth which I dried in the sun, I struck fire and so dried and warmed our wet bodies; and then skinned the goat and having found a small brass pot we boiled some of her. Our drink was brackish water. Bread we had none. There we remained till the Monday following; when about three of the clock in the afternoon, in a boat that came that way, we went off that desolate island, which I named after my name—Thacher's Woe—and the rock Avery his fall, to the end that their fall and loss and mine own might be had in perpetual remembrance. In the isle lieth buried the body of my cousin's eldest daughter, whom I found dead on the shore. On the Tuesday following, in the afternoon, we arrived at Marblehead.

Eventually, a pair of lighthouses were built on Thacher Island in 1771, the last of the colonial lighthouses built under British rule. They stand at 124 feet tall and can be seen very well from the shores of Rockport and Gloucester. From the towers, you can see the skyline of Boston to the south and the mountains of Maine to the northwest. Just about a half mile offshore from Thacher Island is an iron pole sticking out of the water, which marks the Londoner Ledge, which has claimed hundreds of vessels, most of which were traveling between Boston and London in the early 1700s.

The sixty-four-acre island is now part nature preserve, and there are opportunities to camp there in the summer. You will find a small museum and walking trail. Jeannette Haynes worked as a keeper on the island, and she collected sea glass from the island over thirteen years. She made a beautiful tableau of the lighthouses with the sea glass on an old salvaged window from the principal keeper's house on the island. It can be seen in the Thacher Island visitor center. She even found a piece of a German glass float that dated approximately to 1910 on the island. The island is accessible by kayak or small boats (under appropriate weather and sea conditions). During the summer months, the Thacher Island Association operates a boat out of Rockport.

Gloucester

To hold a piece of sea glass from a beach in Gloucester, there are many tales that could be told about its origins from this storied seaport. A fishing outpost was established in 1623 in what was to be Gloucester; however, the

The crashing waves along the coast of Gloucester toss up more than just seaweed and stones.

settlement was abandoned three years later, as the land was not conducive to farming. Slowly, people returned, and some historians report that the fishing schooner was invented in Gloucester in 1713. By the time of the American Revolution, there were over 140 fishing vessels that called this port home, and many of those ships turned to privateering to survive during the challenging days of the Revolution. By the end of the eighteenth century, the fishing fleet had begun to bounce back as waterfront improvements were made to support the fishing industry.

On December 15, 1839, a severe hurricane slammed into Gloucester Harbor, and the catastrophic event was detailed in a printed pamphlet of the day:

> *The calamities we have recorded were nothing in comparison to those which happened at Gloucester. The harbor was supposed to be very secure, and at the commencement of the storm a great many vessels, especially coasters, put in there for shelter. Unfortunately, instead of anchoring in the inner harbor, as far at least as Five Pound Island, or in the South East harbor, in both which places the holding ground is good and the anchorage well sheltered,*

they generally anchored just north of Ten Pound Island and Ten Pound Ledge, where they were right in the teeth of the current of wind rushing in a gale from S.E. or N.N.E., between Rocky Neck and the Fort; in the range of the under-tow rolling over Dog Bar; and on very poor holding ground. Of course the most of them dragged ashore. Such a scene of terrific and horrible ruin has not been witnessed in that harbor within the memory of the oldest resident, a man 104 years of age, who has always lived there.

More than fifty vessels were either driven ashore, dismasted, or carried to sea, and the loss of lives could not have fallen short of fifty. From one end of the beach to the other, nothing could be seen but pieces of broken wrecks; planks and spars shattered into a thousand splinters; ropes and sails parted and rent; flour, fish, lumber, and a hundred other kinds of lading and furniture, soaked and broken; with here and there a mangled and naked body of some poor mariner; and in one instance that of a woman lashed to the windlass-bits of a Coastline schooner, lay along the beach, while off thirty yards, with the surf breaking over them every moment and freezing in the air, lay nearly a score of lost vessels; all together forming a picture which it is in vain to attempt to copy in words.

In the Midst of this scene of terror, the hardy fishermen of Cape Ann fully proved that a sailor's jacket seldom covers a craven heart. They manned two boats, the Custom House boat and the Van Buren, and fearlessly risked their lives for the safety of their fellow creatures. Vessel after vessel was visited by them; they made their way over the tops of mountain-waves, and through the gaping chasms of the hungry waters; and from the very teeth of greedy death plucked many a poor, despairing, and exhausted fellow, bringing him safe to shore. Excellent, generous men! We would we could record all their names, that posterity might approve and emulate their deeds of daring.

In 1830, much of the downtown area of the city burned in a massive fire. It is easy to identify the area of the fire in the historic West End, as it was rebuilt to be fire resistant using granite and brick. A second major fire in 1864 destroyed 103 wooden buildings and houses that lined the harbor. Two ships were destroyed in that fire as well. A three-alarm fire destroyed the massive Surfside Hotel that stood along the harbor in October 1914. Today, this hardworking harbor remains busy throughout the year, and there are deep-sea tuna boats, lobster boats and fishing boats, along with several fish factories that surround the harbor.

The welcoming waterfront esplanade has a variety of memorials and tablets that share the deep losses and memories that this community collectively

The historic promenade overlooks Gloucester Harbor and leads to Pavilion Beach, a popular beachcombing spot.

shares. The twelve-foot bronze and granite Gloucester Fishermen's Wives Memorial depicts a woman and her two children watching for the husband's ships to return to the harbor. Along that path is the Gloucester Fishermen's Memorial Statue, which is dedicated to the ten thousand Gloucester fishermen who have lost their lives at sea.

Located along the esplanade, Pavilion Beach has an abundance of sea glass, pottery, porcelain and even dark purple lightbulb insulators from the early twentieth century floating in on the tide. Industrial fragments and

Pavilion Beach in Gloucester is best explored when the tide is low, giving the explorer more area to wander and make discoveries.

shards from various types of commercial glass can sometimes be found along the shore here as well. On any given day, you won't be alone beachcombing here, no matter what the weather brings. Check the calendar before you plan your visit, as there are some major events that take place here throughout the year. In June, during St. Peter's Fiesta, the greased pole challenge brings out quite a huge audience. Local men will venture out onto a greased telephone pole from the beach over the harbor to bring back the flag that is at the end. The blessing of the fleet also takes place during the festival, which is named for the patron saint of fishermen.

SALEM

Founded in 1626, Salem, Massachusetts, continues to draw people from around the world with its captivating history and modern-day interpretation of the infamous witchcraft trials. The settlement was originally known as

Naumkeag, but it was changed to Salem, which is derived from the Hebrew word for peace. In 1637, the first Salem ship sailed to the West Indies to trade salted cod. Between 1799 and 1879, over 7,900 voyages to foreign ports sailed from Salem. It has been said that Salem ships traded "with more different peoples in Asia, Africa, South America and the islands of the sea than the ships of all other American ports put together." Salem privateering history was unrivaled, with over 150 vessels that captured nearly 450 British ships. The architecture throughout Salem reflects the rich history of successful maritime trade with an abundance of stately captains' houses.

Societies and museums in Salem contain curious items and artifacts that traders brought back with them from ports all around the globe. The East India Marine Society (which is now part of the Peabody Essex Museum) was established in 1799, and the members were master mariners who had navigated the seas beyond Cape Horn. Some of the interesting items that are in the museum collection are a cup and saucer owned by Napoleon, a handcrafted eighty-gun ship made out of soup bones by a prisoner at Dartmoor in England and underwear made from reindeer hair in Lapland, all of which were brought back with Salem mariners from their worldly travels.

The nineteenth century saw a decline in the shipping trade because the harbor was not as deep as other ports in the Northeast. In the introduction of *The Scarlet Letter* by Nathaniel Hawthorne, published in 1850, he wrote that Derby Wharf "is now burdened with decayed wooden warehouses, and exhibits few or no symptoms of commercial life; except, perhaps, a bark or brig, half-way down its melancholy length."

There are a couple of options for the patient sea glass searcher in Salem. One location is hiding in plain sight along the waterfront. Winter Island has a long history and was home to the first shipyard and public house (tavern) in the seventeenth century. There were several wharves, and the island also had an active fort for over 250 years. In 1799, the frigate the USS *Essex* was built and launched here; the ship was the largest ever built in Salem. One section of Winter Island is known as Execution Hill, where there were four public hangings between 1772 and 1821.

The lighthouse on the island was built in 1871, and in 1933, the Coast Guard Air Station Base was opened. Fort Pickering was no longer being used by the time the base was closed in 1968; however, the bunkers are still visible. Many buildings had been abandoned, and broken glass is scattered across the island. Today, the island is owned by the city, which maintains a

Winter Island in Salem, Massachusetts, has many curious layers of history and is a fun place to beachcomb.

public park and campground on the property. When the tide is low, there are two pebbly beaches to explore here. In season, there is a fee to go out onto the island, but the views across the South Channel and Salem Harbor along with the sea glassing make it well worth it.

Another beach in Salem that is worth a visit is in another off-the-beaten-path area called Forest River Park. Pioneer Village, which opened as a living history museum in 1930 as part of Salem's three-hundred-year anniversary, is nearby. The park has seen many recent renovations, and there is ample parking, a pool and lots of shoreline worth exploring here.

Scituate

The earliest notice of a settlement at Scituate dates to 1628. In 1633, the "Men of Kent," who came from that county in England, laid out the house lots and early pathways. One of the earliest shipyards in town dates to 1650, and there is a series of brooks and rivers that were navigated alongside places known as "gravelly beach" and "sunken rocks." There was even an area known as the New Harbour Marshes that were known for round, polished pebbles that followed the waterways to the sea.

A lighthouse was built in 1811 with two steady lights, one red and one white, marked Cedar Point. During the War of 1812, two Redcoat-filled barges from a British ship of war were seen just offshore. The lighthouse keeper's young daughters Abigail and Rebecca Bates reportedly grabbed a fife and drum and hid behind a thick cluster of cedar trees. The way they played their instruments was said to be so convincing that the British mistook them for an entire regiment and made a hasty retreat. The girls have gone down in history as the "Army of Two." Locals have said that fife and drum music can be heard on some nights from the grounds, and on occasion, the spirits of the girls can be seen in the shadows of the lighthouse tower. The family that moved into the keeper's house in January 1970 told the *Boston Globe* that they were eager to meet the ghosts and they thought a haunted lighthouse was a great place to live.

The early Scituate waterfront looked very different from today, as there was a sandbar at the entrance to the harbor. The maximum high tide depth was ten feet, with a depth of two and a half feet at mean low water. Plus, there were many sunken boulders that were hazardous for the mariner to navigate, and there was little to no protection for the settlement from severe ocean storms. By 1903, the U.S. Army Corps of Engineers had built two jetties and dredged the area to create the harbor currently in use.

Hundreds of ships were built in Scituate from the 1670s to the 1950s. There were many highly skilled boat builders who gained a reputation for their well-built vessels. Men like Captain "Bill" Bates were known to go out as volunteers on lifeboat crews after severe northeasters would drive boats ashore—and sometimes into each other. In May 1855, Captain Bill saved two women who were left to drift away helplessly after a boat collision at Thacher Island in Rockport. The wind and current sent them way down the coast to Scituate. It was described as a harrowing experience trying to save them from the wreckage of the schooner. On another occasion, he saved six men from the schooner *Abigail Healy*, which wrecked on Third Cliff Beach. Shipwrecks in Scituate were numerous; between 1807 and 1919, there are ninety-five documented wrecks. Severe weather conditions along with navigating the dangerous and rocky underwater landscape were largely to blame. Scituate was also a harbor of refuge where many ships would drop their anchors while waiting out severe weather in Boston Harbor.

There are several popular beaches in Scituate that also have a great view of Cape Cod Bay, such as Humarock and the quickly eroding Peggotty Beach. In 1695, the first recorded shipwreck happened on a rocky ledge just one mile offshore of Minot Beach. Over the next fifty years, eighty ships and approximately four hundred lives were lost in the surrounding waters. Shortly after 1754, the outcropping of rock was named Minots Ledge after a Boston merchant named George Minot lost his ship there. A lighthouse was proposed in the 1840s; however, the task of constructing one on the ledge proved to be a near impossible undertaking.

It took two years to build an unusual skeleton-style lighthouse that was able to somewhat withstand the wind and waves while secured to a rock. Nine iron pilings were cemented into the rock, and the thirty-ton lightkeeper's house was built precariously on top of it, with the total height of the structure being seventy-five feet. The first lighthouse keeper complained how the building would sway back and forth in storms, sometimes displacing the dishes on the kitchen table, and he eventually left his post. On April 16, 1851, a storm took down the lighthouse after midnight with two men inside. On the front page of the May 2, 1851 *Boston Evening Transcript*, a poem was published described the harrowing event. An excerpt in part reads:

Wo [sic] *for the mournful Minot Ledge;*
Her crown of light has fled;
And they who lit her beacon fires
Are with the ocean's dead.
Through the wild hours of midnight deep,
They kept the watch-tower lone,—
But when the murky morning broke,
The waves had claimed their own.

As dawn approached at 4:00 a.m., reports of debris from the lighthouse were observed on Minot Beach, "strewed all around, fragments of the building. Parts of the residence room and of the lantern itself, were seen on the beach," along with bedding and clothing. Soon after, a Gloucester fisherman found a message in a bottle from the two lighthouse keepers that read, "The beacon cannot last any longer. She is shaking a good three feet each way as I write. God bless you all."

A lightship was stationed near the ledge for the next nine years while another lighthouse was built, which also had its share of troubles. In 1860, the lighthouse was lit, and it has become known as the "I Love You" lighthouse, as the beacon flashes in a 1-4-3 cycle. The current lighthouse has been rumored to be haunted by the keepers who were lost in 1851. Later lighthouse keepers and passing fishermen have reported seeing apparitions of a floating lantern and hearing men yelling and the ringing of the old lighthouse bell.

The churning of the tides in Scituate is legendary. Chances are that during the worst winter storms, the weather forecasters will be broadcasting live from the town. The Blizzard of '78 left its mark on the town, destroying 190 homes and severely damaging nearly 400 others. A 2018 nor'easter showered houses and property with ocean debris in piles as high as eight feet from the force of twenty-seven-foot waves, powered by eighty-mile-per-hour winds. The Scituate Historical Society has an exhibit of a Tabasco sauce bottle embedded into a wooden ship's plank as a testament to the force of the sea. With patience and persistence, an exploration of Cedar Point and the beaches of Scituate can yield finds buried within the changing layers of this beautiful coastal town.

Boston Harbor

Exploring the beaches around Boston Harbor can be fun and rewarding for the intrepid beachcomber who doesn't mind going off-season and who is patient and thorough in their explorations. There are two beaches that are great for beachcombing in the early morning or during the off-season from September to November. Carson Beach and the M Street Beach are located along William J. Day Boulevard overlooking Dorchester Bay. Treasures discovered here can date back to the 1930s and 1940s, during the heyday of the beach, or you might find glass and artifacts that reach back into the eighteenth and nineteenth centuries of maritime trade.

Over the years, there have been several projects to clean the waterfront, and the beach area is the best it's been in nearly one hundred years. The nearby Curley Community Center (once a bathhouse) was reopened in the summer of 2023 after a $31 million renovation that celebrates the building's historic Art Deco architecture. The center offers recreation activities, events and workout rooms and is a perfect addition to a beachcombing visit. Parking is limited, and there are metered spaces and some small parking lots in the area. Be sure to read the signs and keep track of your time here.

Deer Island, Winthrop

Deer Island in Winthrop is a gateway into Boston Harbor, and its history and legacy are quite compelling. To beachcomb here is to sift through the many layers of the past and in the shadows of the ghosts of the island inhabitants who have long since passed. The island was so named in 1634 due to the large number of deer that were seen grazing in the high forests and grassy glades that used to be the landscape. A narrow channel used to separate the island from the mainland, but the Hurricane of 1938 filled it in.

During King Philip's War in the winter of 1675, Native peoples were exiled to the island with no food and no supplies. It has been estimated that 500 of them died there due to inhospitable conditions. Deer Island was also a quarantine station until 1671, when the passengers of an arriving ship were stricken with smallpox. In the 1840s, over 4,800 Irish immigrants were sent to the island with what was referred to as "ship fever" (typhus and other ailments) that they had contracted aboard what were known as "coffin ships." The epidemic was so formidable that it even infected the staff of doctors and

Unusual finds can be gathered along the shore of Deer Island, which overlooks the Boston skyline.

nurses who cared for them in the hospital on the island. Approximately 850 people died on the island in what is known as the "Famine Years" between 1847 and 1850. In 1852, an almshouse, school and farm were established on the island.

Eventually, a reform school and prison were built in the late nineteenth century. The prison was closed and demolished in 1991 to make way for the ultra-modern wastewater treatment plant that would help clean up Boston Harbor. The island was also home to Fort Dawes, a military defense that was built in 1907 and was blown up and demolished in the 1990s as part of the revitalization of the island. Today, there are upward of 1,200 people who are buried on the island, with several recent memorials and monuments that help to tell their stories. There are many legends that the island is haunted by the spirits of its past as a reminder of the history, intent that it's not ever forgotten.

To get to Deer Island, take Shirley Street to Tafts Avenue in Winthrop and follow the signs. There are two parking areas at the entrance to the island. A two-and-a-half-mile Harborwalk loops around the island, where there are a few gravel beaches to explore. Be mindful of the tides and heed no-trespassing areas. The variety of items and artifacts to discover here while beachcombing includes bits of pottery and dishware that dates to the early twentieth century, and researching those finds can be quite fun. The unobstructed views of the Boston skyline are some of the best, so you may want to bring along your camera as well.

Fort Taber, New Bedford

Bedford Village was originally part of the Dartmouth settlement in Massachusetts and was officially incorporated in 1787. The community suffered greatly in a lesser-known raid that took place during the American Revolution. On September 4, 1778, four thousand British soldiers on 40 ships overtook the village to put a stop to privateering and to bring commerce to a standstill. They burned and destroyed 34 ships, numerous warehouses, wharves and several homes. It was reported that the fires in what became known as Grey's raids were seen for twenty miles around. After the War of 1812, New Bedford quickly became one of the leading whaling ports in the world, and by 1857, there were 329 whale ships registered to New Bedford. When the whaling industry slowed down, business entrepreneurs, manufactured goods and the railroad kept people employed and the port vibrant.

As the city flourished, a coastal defense fortification grew with it. Originally known as the Old Stone Fort, it evolved into Fort Rodman and eventually Fort Taber. The fort, which overlooks Buzzard's Bay, was active through World War II with several batteries and fixed mounted guns. Eventually, the property was taken over by the city, and a fifty-acre waterfront park with walking trails and playgrounds was established. A lighthouse that was rebuilt and renovated over the years is also part of the fort and most recently was renovated in 2001. A military museum that hosts historic reenactments can be found on site as well.

A loop trail goes around the outer edge of the park, and there is quite a bit of beach here to explore for sea glass. There is a long pier that reaches out into the harbor and is perfect for getting a view across the bay and back to the fort. Shipwrecks are still being discovered and extensively documented in New Bedford's deep-water harbor, making beachcombing finds especially intriguing. You may find that a day trip is be the ideal way to spend some relaxing time enjoying the shore and the historic fort.

CHAPTER 7

RHODE ISLAND

And ye who one brief hour of summer roam
These winding shores to breathe in the bracing breeze,
And feel the freedom of the skies and seas.
—"Aquidneck," Charles Timothy Brooks, 1848

Rhode Island may be the smallest state, measuring thirty-seven miles wide and forty-eight miles long, yet it boasts over four hundred miles of coastline. The first of the colonies to declare its independence, the state was originally called the Providence Plantations. Roger Williams spoke out against the magistrates of Massachusetts and was declared a heretic for his beliefs on religious freedom. The maritime history here is quite rich, literally and figuratively, with some of the most opulent summer cottages in the region located in popular Newport.

There are soft, smooth sandy beaches and rough and tumbling rocky coves to be explored here. The beach views never disappoint; from hardworking lobster boats to world-class racing yachts, you are in for a treat watching the ever-moving seafaring traffic in the background of your beachcombing adventures. The multitude of forts, museums and majestic lighthouses will beckon you to stay longer and become acquainted with the history here. You will want to wrap up your day of collecting treasures at a local restaurant, where you can find a variety of fresh and delicious seafood or partake in a frosty Del's lemonade. What better place to take off on a sea glass adventure than a place called the Ocean State.

Jamestown

The town of Jamestown is situated on Conanicut Island, which is just one mile wide and approximately nine miles long. The open waters of the Atlantic Ocean known as Block Island Sound wash the rugged southern shores of Jamestown. It was originally the summer camping ground for the Narragansett Indian tribe and was named for the chief who permitted English settlers to graze their sheep on the island. The history and legends of this island are numerous, enriching any visit.

In 1695, Captain Thomas Paine built a house on the north end of the island. He was a successful privateer and a friend of Captain Kidd. Paine's adventures on the sea started in 1647, and by the 1660s, he had become notorious, having raided several ships and ports on the Caribbean Sea. Paine was quite a bold man who sailed into Newport Harbor in 1683 with a vessel he had captured and presented forged papers for it. The British tax collector in Boston attempted to seize the ship, but the governor of Rhode Island, William Coddington, refused, saying the papers were in order. Captain Paine was able to keep his prize and settled in Jamestown. Just a few years later, during King William's War, Block Island was attacked by French privateers. With two sloops and ninety men in his fleet, Captain Paine became a local hero when he was able to drive off the five French vessels and two hundred men.

The captain entertained a number of buccaneers at his house, called Cajacet, in Jamestown. One of his visitors was none other than the infamous pirate Captain William Kidd. According to legend, Captain Kidd left a great deal of his treasures with Captain Paine before he headed to Boston, where he was going to turn himself in, expecting a pardon. When he arrived in Boston, he was imprisoned, and Kidd's wife, Sarah, who was also imprisoned, sent a letter to Captain Paine asking him for twenty-eight ounces of gold to help them in their time of need and told Paine that he could keep the rest. Paine did indeed send the money, but it was of no use. Captain Kidd was sent to London and executed by hanging in 1701. It was believed that Paine buried the treasure at his home in Jamestown. A twist on the legend is that in the 1950s, workmen digging in the yard of the house left abruptly and didn't come back. Upon closer examination of the site, a gold coin was found where they were digging.

Life on the island was quiet until the American Revolution hit, and on December 10, 1775, the British landed in Jamestown and confiscated livestock, causing many islanders to flee to Newport. The British occupation of the island ended in 1779. After the Revolution ended, peaceful tranquility and farming returned to the island. The nineteenth century brought change to the rural atmosphere as it became a destination for vacationers from Newport. Hotels, boardinghouses and summer homes followed.

During the Hurricane of 1938, the headlines of the *Newport Mercury* reported on September 23: "Nine persons die in Jamestown Storm. Waterfront almost wiped out, two ferry boats blown ashore during height of gale." The story went on to describe the incredible scene:

> *The White Nook restaurant was blown across the street, Alfred Richardson's Garage was blown away, the Newport Coal Company office was tossed over and numerous buildings had roofs blown off and were otherwise damaged, while hundreds of trees were torn up by the roots. The beach pavilion was washed away, and all over the island there was evidence of the storm today.*

The landscape changed again when the old hotels like the Bay View and the Harbor View Inn were razed in the 1980s and replaced with condominiums.

At the southern end of the island is Beavertail lighthouse, which occupies a rocky, windswept point. As early as 1705, there was a watch house built on the site, and the current lighthouse there was built in 1856. The lighthouse is located within Beavertail State Park and is home to a museum that includes the history of not only the lighthouse but Narragansett Bay as well.

Fort Wetherill State Park, situated on one-hundred-foot-high granite cliffs across the water from Fort Adams State Park, is a former coastal defense battery and training camp and a busy scuba diving site where there is a small beach area that is worthy of a quick visit. On the eastern edge of the park is the Submarine Mine and Cable Facility. Some of the buildings date back to the early 1900s, and the long, one-story building was a submarine mine warehouse that was built in 1940. There are some small sections of shore here that can be explored.

The Park Dock is a great location for beachcombing, as this was the location for a wharf and steamboat landing for travel among Providence, Jamestown and Newport. It is located at the end of Broad Street off East Shore Road. This little-known, quiet, rocky beach has a spectacular view of Narragansett Bay and the entrance to Mount Hope Bay.

Another great spot for unearthing sea glass in Jamestown is Mackerel Cove. The pavilion that stood at this beach at one time had one hundred roomy bathhouses and even a dance hall. The structure was reduced to a set of stairs during the Hurricane of 1938. The water on this beach is shallow and crystal clear. Access to the beach is free. Parking is limited, and there is a fee in season.

COMPASS ROSE BEACH, NORTH KINGSTOWN

The history of North Kingstown goes back to 1641, and the efforts to preserve and honor the area's agricultural history are evident during a drive through this community. There are a handful of beaches to explore in town, but the Compass Rose Beach, located at Quonset Point, may yield your best beachcombing finds. The site has layers of history that can be found in some of the discoveries on the beach. During the Spanish-American War, Rhode Island established a militia campground on Quonset Point. In 1938, this was a training site for the navy's fighter squadrons in the leadup to World War II. By the 1970s, the military operations had been scaled back, and eventually, several manufacturing plants opened on the site. Compass Rose Beach is an old seaplane beach that faces the west passage of Narragansett Bay.

The beach is located along Roger Williams Way and is adjacent to the Quonset Airport. There is a very small parking lot, which limits the number of people on the beach. There are strong waves, which with the grainy sand create the perfect conditions for sea glass. There are a lot of tumbled brick fragments all over the beach, which are perfect for collecting or stacking small cairns out of. Your pockets may not be totally filled with glass here, but it's a fun place to explore and find some treasures without the challenge of crowds.

EASTON'S BEACH, NEWPORT

Located on Memorial Boulevard in Newport, Rhode Island, Easton's Beach offers beachcombers a truly opulent view of some of the famous Gilded Age mansions. The beach is named for Nicholas Easton, who was one of the original settlers of Newport and later governor of Rhode Island. Skilled tradesmen, merchants and colonial artisans lived in the area just beyond the beach known as Easton's Point, which is a designated Historic District of Newport.

On August 9, 1857, the *Newport Daily News* reported the following scene at Easton's Beach:

The southern breeze blew softly from the tremulous horizon upon the shining sands, long lines of carriages sped swiftly and noiselessly over the smooth, sloping shore, which the receding tide had relinquished to the equal delight of horses and riders. Amid the rolling foam, or flitting gaily to and from their cars, were troops of bathers, of all possible sizes, clad in robes of many shapes and colors, and presenting, generally, a bewildering and fantastic spectacle. Happiness beamed in a thousand faces.

Also known as First Beach, it was advertised in the early twentieth century as the "coolest place to spend the day." A massive gateway led to a sprawling boardwalk where you would find several shops, pavilions and amusements. The massive entrance and design of the structure at that point looked like an oversized Mediterranean villa. The Old Mill Roller Coaster thrilled riders, who would afterward quench their thirst on a five-cent soda from the Hygeia Cafe while listening to Davino's Brass Band. For those who were looking for something unique, they could cool themselves at the Roman Gardens saltwater pool.

The fury of the Hurricane of 1938 leveled everything at Easton's Beach. The city described the scene of destruction "as if it never existed." The carousel and the roller coaster, which drew people from as far away as the South Shore of Massachusetts, were ripped apart as the massive waves tore

Easton Beach in Newport offers a view of the spectacular mansions along Cliff Walk while beachcombing.

at the boardwalk. The pavilion was rebuilt some time later in a humbler fashion, but it seemed as though the golden age of amusements was gone forever.

The rocky edges of the beach are the best places to look for sea glass here in the off season. If you are looking for a variety of sea glass or artifacts, this may not be the best choice; however, if you are looking to do a little beachcombing before exploring the Cliff Walk (which is a stunning scenic path that trails behind the mansions), you might really enjoy your visit. Should you pick up a few treasures here, they may connect you to the bustling heyday of this beach's history.

FORT ADAMS, NEWPORT

Named for President John Adams, Fort Adams is strategically situated at the entrance to Newport Harbor and Narragansett Bay. The original fort that was constructed here was built in 1799 and was active until the War of 1812. Construction on the current fort started in 1824, and it took thirty-three years to complete. One of the largest forts in America, it spans over 105 acres, and it once housed sixty-eight cannons and 2,400 soldiers. The fort was never attacked, nor did it see battle, and it stands as a reminder of how strong and intimidating our defenses were.

The history of the fort is not without its share of legends, lore and tragedy, however. After a Fourth of July celebration in 1819, Private William Kane was shot and killed by Private William G. Cornell over an extra ration of rum. Private Cornell was tried and convicted of first-degree murder and was sentenced to be executed by hanging. At the eleventh hour, a last-minute pardon came in from President James Monroe, stopping the execution. It was believed to have been brought on by a plea from Cornell's mother.

On January 19, 1925, Mary Gleason, an Irish immigrant who worked as a maid, had an appointment at the fort to meet a man for a date. The night was windy, and the temperature hovered around nine degrees. She became lost in an abandoned area of the fort and fell off the exterior wall into a deep ditch. She was found several days later frozen and covered in snow. Although a man claiming to be her former boyfriend confessed to the crime of pushing her to her death, it was determined that he wasn't even in town when it happened. The ruling on the case was accidental death, yet there are many conspiracy theories around what really happened.

Designed to be the most heavily armed fort in America, Fort Adams stands at the entrance to bustling Newport Harbor.

There have been quite a few deaths at the fort that go back to accidents that happened during the early years when the fort was being built. Accounts of suicides, bodies washed ashore from shipwrecks and several murders cast an ominous shadow over the history of the fort. In 1918, during the Spanish flu outbreak, five residents of the fort died onsite. Within the fortification walls is a cemetery with over two hundred people buried there, including William Brenton, who was governor of Rhode Island and died in 1675. Over the years, many visitors to the fort have reported ghostly sightings and experiences. Full-bodied apparitions, disembodied voices, mysterious knocks and even gravel-throwing spirits are part of the haunted history here. Ghost tours and investigations have regularly taken place at the fort over the years.

There are a few small beach areas that are perfect to explore surrounding the fort. Head over to Lookout Point, which has incredible views of the harbor, and you'll find two areas that are ideal to spend some time combing through the sand. Take the Fort Adams Bay walk, which is a two-and-a-half-mile trail along the shore that loops around the fort, to discover other little pocket beach areas to investigate. Be sure to check the fort's schedule in advance, as there are many events that take place here in season, like the Newport Jazz Festival, which draws in thousands of people. You may want to schedule a ghost tour at the fort after beachcombing to see who may have been watching over your shoulder while you were making your discoveries.

WALLEY BEACH, BRISTOL

Bristol is situated on a ten-square-mile peninsula shaped like a lobster claw, with Narragansett Bay to the west and Mount Hope Bay to the east. John Walley was one of the original proprietors of what was known as Mount Hope Neck and Poppasquash Neck in the seventeenth century. He was a wealthy Boston merchant who, with three other men, drew up the plans for the layout of the town and its harbor. The settlement was well established and grew quickly. Bristol's early shipping trade included the export of livestock, fish and lumber and the import of furs, tea, coffee, textiles, china and manufactured goods. Five rum distilleries prospered along the waterfront in the eighteenth century. Originally under the jurisdiction of Massachusetts, Bristol became part of Rhode Island in 1747. During the American Revolution, the British raided Bristol twice, burning the church and many boats in the harbor.

It was said that a forest of ships' masts dominated Bristol's skyline at one time, and there were at least twenty wharves that extended out into the harbor. By the early nineteenth century, most of the occupations held by the residents of the town were connected in one form or another to the sea. As the century progressed, the waterfront activities switched to manufacturing with a focus on textile mills, rubber products and shipbuilding.

The September gales of 1815 and 1869 were quite destructive to Bristol's waterfront. A series of newly built brick warehouses were filled with merchandise that was washed into the harbor and driven onto the shores by wind and tide. It was reported that the winds had picked up large trees and tossed them around like feathers during the storms. The people of Bristol salvaged what they could from the beaches around the harbor, but the storms caused major losses.

The harbor area is still bustling, and there are historic buildings dotting the shore as far as the eye can see. The Herreshoff Manufacturing Company,

An unexpected place to find sea glass is at Walley Beach Park on Hope Street in Bristol.

which produced steam-powered vessels and world-class sailing yachts from 1878 to 1945, used to stand along the harbor. The nearby Herreshoff Marine Museum preserves the legacy and history of those days. Bristol is also home to America's oldest Fourth of July parade, which began in 1785 and is one of the major events in the community.

A hidden gem for beachcombing, the Walley Street Beach is located off Hope Street (Route 114) and has a tiny parking area adjacent to a small but scenic park. A seawall slopes down to a set of narrow stone steps that lead to the water. The wind blows strong from the southwest toward the shore, and you will often find wind surfers launching here. It is important to visit here at low tide, as the beach areas are small, but the finds are plentiful. The currents and the wind continue to push under-the-sea treasures up from the bottom of the harbor. Be sure to check the corners around the steps, where a lot of debris collects. If you're feeling extra adventurous, bring your kayak and look at Bristol from the water, and you'll get a terrific view of this historic harbor.

Bristol Town Beach

Located on Asylum Road in Bristol is the Town Beach, at the entrance to Colt State Park. This is a fascinating area to explore with a variety of historic chapters to explain the glass that washes ashore on the sandy beach here. Directly across the water is Rocky Point State Park, which was a major amusement park that began in the mid-nineteenth century and closed in 1995. The park was hit hard by the Hurricane of 1938. The book *The Great Hurricane*, published by the *Providence Journal*, described the scene: "Rocky Point, that Mecca of politicians and shore dinner consumers, fell like a house of cards before the southeast fury. The roller coaster was shattered, the great dining hall…was a soggy mass of lumber, a thousand bathing suits hung from the backwoods trees. The oldest and most famous shore resort of the State was no more." While the park reopened and invited guests for several years, shortsighted business deals led to its closure. What was left was sold off, and the state purchased the land and converted it into a public park.

Colt State Park begins where the beach ends and is a breathtaking 464-acre park composed of woodlands and marshland overlooking Narragansett

Located at the edge of Narragansett Bay, Colt State Park spans over 450 acres.

Bristol Town Beach is an ideal place to sift through crushed shells to find sea glass.

Bay. In 1905, Samuel Pomeroy Colt, nephew of the famous gunmaker, purchased old farmlands on Poppasquash Neck and allowed the public to have access to the land under an agreement he made with the town. There are several magnificent structures on the property, including the shingled casino building that was used for large gatherings and parties in its early days. The grounds include numerous pathways, nature trails and picnic areas. It's an ideal escape after a morning of beachcombing at the Town Beach. The beach is quite sandy and has a multitude of broken shells, so be sure to wear shoes. Because the sand is gray, clear or white sea glass blends in quite easily. There is a plethora strewn across the beach from tiny to nickel sized. You might want to select a spot and just slowly sift through the sands to find your treasures. The tideline here yields some good finds on certain days as well.

CHAPTER 8

CONNECTICUT

The sea was in a frolicsome mood to-day and tumbled the pebbles within her reach across the sands of the curving beach.
—Arthur Cleveland Hall, Connecticut Quarterly, *1898*

Connecticut offers over six hundred miles of coastline to be enjoyed, with a variety of seaside parks and busy industrial centers. A large part of the state's coastline is on Long Island Sound, which is an estuary where fresh water and salt water mix that was formed over twenty-two thousand years ago during the ice age. Historic seaside towns like Mystic and Stonington bring visitors back to the grand and hardworking days of ship and sail with beautiful sea captains' homes.

Connecticut is home to some terrific museums, like the Mystic Seaport Museum, where you never know what amazing story or artifact you might discover. The Connecticut River Museum in Essex is a great way to get an understanding of the many vessels built there and the maritime history of the area. At the Museum on the Green operated by the Glastonbury Historical Society, you can learn about Glastonbury Glass Factory and find some great examples of Wassuc glass, which would have been crafted in the early 1800s. Inkstands, utility bottles, snuff bottles and flasks were made by Wassuc and were known for their free-blown, pattern-molded and mold-brown green glass. Taking the time to get to know the seaside cities and towns in Connecticut will help explorers understand the best places to find and identify time-worn sea treasures.

A few examples of Wassuc glass on display at the Glastonbury Historical Society in Connecticut.

SEASIDE PARK, BRIDGEPORT

Bridgeport is known as Park City, and its waterfront comprises five peninsulas, several creeks and rivers. Seaside Park is a unique 375-acre park with two and a half miles of waterfront in this urban oasis on Long Island Sound. P.T. Barnum was one of the most famous residents of Bridgeport and was instrumental in purchasing the land that became the park. Nathaniel Wheeler and Colonel William Noble joined Barnum in his efforts to set aside the waterfront land to become a park in the 1860s. Frederick Law Olmsted and Calvert Vaux led the architectural firm that was retained to draw up the plans for the park. The same visionary firm had created the design for Central Park in Manhattan. The park was dedicated in 1876 and served the rapidly growing population of the city.

Seaside Park was the epicenter of gatherings and events in the city with a horse track, festivals, camps and all sorts of recreational opportunities. From bathing suit parades to presidential addresses, the park thrived with

Seaside Park in Bridgeport, Connecticut, has such a long shoreline to be explored, visitors are sure to find sea glass quickly and easily.

welcoming walking paths, shade trees and ponds to enjoy. Olmsted said that it was "a capital place for a drive or walk...a fine dressy promenade." Steamboat travel brought visitors and day trippers between New York and Bridgeport.

A total of 140 shipwrecks rest beneath the waters of Long Island Sound, and an area known as "wreck alley" is where schooners, steamboats and yachts slowly deteriorate over time. A wooden Chinese schooner sank in sixty-five feet of water in the late 1800s, and ballast and debris are scattered across the ocean floor over thirty feet. People have reported collecting pieces of porcelain fragments from the schooner. Another wreck lying in the waters of the harbor is the three-masted schooner *Myronus*, which was built in 1865 in Ellsworth, Maine. On August 12, 1907, the schooner collided with the steamer *Tennessee*. The crew of four was lost, and the ship sank. Three canal barges, the *Priscilla Dailey*, *Elmer S. Dailey* and *Berkshire No. 7*, were used for the transportation of people and goods. In 1974, the dock the barges were tied to was submerged in water, and the three barges went down together and are also underneath the harbor. Surveys by the NOAA and maps are still being drawn of what they are discovering in the depths of the waters of the sound.

From the 1980s to 1993, on the eastern side of the harbor was a thirty-five-foot-high pile of trash and construction debris known as "Mount Trashmore." The trash was tumbling and seeping into the harbor slowly and posed a danger to wildlife. The pile was cleared out in the mid-1990s by the City of Bridgeport and the Department of Environmental Protection. This cleanup was an important step in keeping out trash and contaminants from the waterfront environment.

The beaches here are a wonderland of discoveries by the handful. The glass is quite seasoned and sugared, and lots of colors can be found easily. Parking is convenient, and there is good access to the beaches with long sidewalks and ramps. Millions of dollars have been spent in recent years adding bathhouses and showers. Fairweather lighthouse stands at the far end of the park and is connected by a stone jetty that you can walk on. If you choose to take the walk, be careful because the jetty disappears at high tide. There are some great areas to explore around the pier near the jetty.

Silver Sands State Park, Milford

The scenic boardwalk that goes for one-quarter mile over the peaceful marsh to Silver Sands Beach in Milford is tranquil and most welcoming. There are 297 acres of woods, dunes and beach to be enjoyed here. This area became a park in the 1960s, a few years after Hurricane Diane swept through and destroyed seventy-five homes on this site. Part of the property that became the park was used as a town dump until the late 1970s. Charles Island is just across from the beach, and its mysterious history might be another one of the reasons why there is sea glass to be found here. The 14-acre island was owned by the Native peoples, and it has been suggested that there was a large wigwam on the island. The island was said to have been sold to a man named George Hubbard by Native American chiefs of the Wepawug and Paugussett for six coats, ten blankets, twelve hatchets, twelve hoes, two dozen knives and one mirror. In the 1650s, a man named Charles Deal (for whom the island is named) purchased the island to grow tobacco, which ended up being unsuccessful.

In 1835, the beautiful island inspired a man named Major John Harris to build a summer residence there. Eventually, the island changed hands and became a resort in the mid-nineteenth century called the Island House, which boasted seventy-five rooms and attracted guests who traveled by steamship. An aquarium could be found on the island that billed itself as the largest in the country and featured one of P.T. Barnum's trained seals. The owner of the resort, Elizur Pritchard, died on Thanksgiving 1860 while walking on the breakwater from the beach out to the island. His daughter sold the property a few years later, and it became a fish oil and fertilizer plant; it was shut down after a few years because of the stench that it produced. In 1888, the hotel burned to the ground, and the days of grandeur were over.

Stories of shipwrecks, overturned boats and drownings in the waters surrounding the island are part of the history here, too. The *Day* newspaper on February 2, 1886, reported the following:

> *The Fate of the crew of the schooner* Henry C. Gibbs *sunk off of Charles Island, Milford, is still unknown, but it is quite certain that the three men perished in the water on that bitter cold night when the vessel went down. On the morning when the wreck became known men were seen in the rigging, but when assistance went to them they had disappeared. The* Gibbs *was driven into Milford harbor in a terrific gale and sunk during the night. It seems likely that her crew took to the rigging and there remained*

exhausted, then dropped into the sea and perished. The vessel has been raised but no bodies were found.

A religious retreat was opened by the Dominican fathers in 1927 on the island, and the buildings they constructed there were all named after religious saints. There were fourteen cabins on the island and even a kitchen and restaurant in one of the buildings. Just over ten years later, the retreat was closed without explanation, and the buildings were abandoned.

There are a variety of myths and legends about the area. Some believe that Captain Kidd buried some of his treasure on the island, although none has ever been found. Allegedly, a headless ghost surrounded by blue flames appeared when treasure hunters went digging on the island. Some people have even referred to the island as a cursed place. Today, it is a nature preserve and nesting site for birds.

There are mountains of seashells that can be found on Silver Sands Beach, and watching the tides rolling those shells and other shimmering treasures under the boardwalks is mesmerizing. The swift-moving tidal channels leading into the marsh continue to churn up the sands, unearthing what still might be hidden from years ago. The causeway out to Charles Island is tempting and a bit of a hike but comes with a stern warning to be mindful of the tides, as people are regularly stranded on the island. The waters are particularly clear here due to the flourishing mussel beds that are teeming with countless sea stars.

West Haven

The colonial settlement originally known as West Farms in 1648 and later as West Haven started out as part of nearby New Haven. It was a busy shipping and trading port; ships from West Haven sailed to the West Indies and South America for spices, silks, rum, sugar and similar items in return for local timber. West Haven was the town that British troops marched through on the way to burn New Haven on July 5, 1779. The success and contributions of this town are many, including a ship and boat building industry that thrived through World War II. There is a legacy that still can be found in part and in small pieces rolling across the town's scenic beaches.

George Kelsey, a Civil War veteran and entrepreneur, built a 1,500-foot pier along West Haven's waterfront, known as Savin Rock, and a hotel that could host 150 guests to welcome visitors by ferry. Visitors also came to the park via new bustling trolley lines. It was opened in 1870. In the 1890s, electricity came to the growing complex, and there were dazzling light displays, electric fountains and electric trolley cars. In 1910, a large new movie theater was built, but it burned down just three years later. Another massive pier was built in 1922, and you could ride the roller coasters out over the ocean waves. The popularity of Savin Rock continued to grow quickly. It was said that family, friends and people you met along the way were headed to Savin Rock.

There seemed to be such a tremendous number of things to do there, with multiple roller coasters, water chutes, spooky dark rides and mechanical fortunetellers. Bluebeard's Castle Funhouse was a massive structure that seemed larger than life. Spectacular hotels housed visitors who wanted to visit for more than just one day. Fires plagued the park, and the Hurricane of 1938 destroyed the eighty-five-foot-tall roller coaster, the Thunderbolt. Repairs to the park and the building of a new roller coaster brought the crowds back once again. In the 1950s, a section of the park known as Hot Dog Alley was quite famous in the region. It was reported that there was a weekly consumption of 6,700 lobster rolls, 300 gallons of clams and 800 pounds of shrimp, washed down by 360,000 bottles of soda.

By the 1960s, the aging park had become rundown, and much-needed upgrades and repairs fell by the wayside. Illegal activities were a frequent issue for law enforcement, and by 1966, the park had closed for good. Many folks who remember the park still speak about it fondly. Redevelopment plans for the area were not without controversy at the time. Today, West Haven has the largest publicly accessible shoreline in the state of Connecticut along Ocean Avenue. Bradley Point has an accessible boardwalk with several food options if you are looking to try the local flavor. Oak Street Beach is popular with fishermen, as there is a long pier out into the water, and there are a lot of small pebbles and grit to sift through. There are several other beach options along the waterfront, but be sure to find out parking information in advance, as it can be challenging at times in season. Beachcombing in West Haven offers the possibility of picking up a relic of the Savin Rock Amusement Park or some historic treasure from the thrilling shipping past of this town.

Sherwood Island State Park, Westport

The area where Sherwood Island State Park is in Westport was once known as Machamux, which meant "The Beautiful Land," named by the Native peoples, the Pequots. The area developed into a flourishing farm owned by the Sherwood family in the eighteenth century. A gristmill turned in the winds of Long Island Sound for many years. Root vegetables like onions and potatoes were grown here, and oysters flourished and were harvested and shipped to New York.

In the early 1900s, efforts were put forth to establish a state park, and in 1914, property was purchased. An addition was made in 1937, and it is officially Connecticut's oldest state park. There are 234 acres to explore with nature trails, tidal marshes and two beaches to visit. The geology is quite interesting, with three different types of sand on the beaches. There's black sand magnetite, which is an iron oxide. There is a lot of naturally occurring quartz present, accounting for the white sand. The red garnet sand here is ideal for smoothing sea glass because it is naturally abrasive.

On a clear day, the panorama of the New York City skyline comes into sharp view. On site is the 9/11 Living Memorial, with a nine-foot-long granite memorial stone with names carved into it. Beach-found items, including shells and sea glass, rest next to each name on the stone. Inside the pavilion is a sculpture called *Sanctuary* that was crafted out of shards of metal recovered from the Twin Towers. A large, colorful mosaic mural of a tree consisting of pottery, dishware and sea glass can be found on one of the walls of the pavilion.

There is a lot of wildlife in the state park, including geese, and bird-watching is great. You'll find lots of picnic tables, and there is easy beach access. There is a fee to enter the park, so be sure to check the rates before you go. The beach terrain is a bit coarse and there are lots of broken shells, so tread carefully and have fun making your discoveries of sea glass along the shore.

CHAPTER 9
CURATING YOUR COLLECTION

The importance of glass, and the infinite variety of objects to which it is applicable, cannot be exaggerated; indeed, it would be extremely difficult to enumerate its properties, or estimate adequately its value. This, then, transparent substance, so light and fragile, is one of the most essential ministers of science and philosophy and enters so minutely into the concerns of life that it has become indispensable to the daily routine of our business, our wants, and our pleasures.

It admits the sun and excludes the wind, answering the double purpose of transmitting light and preserving warmth; it carries the eye of the astronomer to the remotest regions of space; through the lenses of the microscope it develops new worlds of vitality, which, without its help, must have been but imperfectly known; it renews the sight of the old, and assists the curiosity of the young; it empowers the mariner to descry distant ships, and trace far off shores; the watchman on the cliff to detect the operations of hostile fleets and midnight contrabandists, and the lounger in the opera to make the tour of the circles from his stall; it preserves the light of the beacon from the rush of the tempest, and softens the flame of the lamp upon our tables; it supplies the revel with those charming vessels in whose bright depths we enjoy the color as well as the flavor of our wine; it protects the dial whose movements it reveals; it enables the student to penetrate the wonders of nature, and the beauty to survey the marvels of her person; it reflects, magnifies, and diminishes; as a medium of light and observation its uses are without limit, and as an article of mere embellishment, there is no form into which it may not be moulded, or no object of luxury to which it may not be adapted.

—Harper's Magazine, *February 1851*

O nce you've brought your beach finds home, what is the next step for the little treasures gathered in pockets, baggies, bins and buckets? A fun way to chronicle your adventures is to label your finds with the location found and the date. Taking a picture of your treasures on the beach or along the tideline is a great way to add to the story of your adventure. That information can be entered into a journal or calendar. After some time, you can look back and see what the best days of the year were for treasure seeking and determine which locations yielded the most finds. Additional notes may include the phase of the moon and the time of the tides.

Some people choose to sort their finds by color, size or sugared quality, while others separate the porcelain and pottery pieces. A small and simple light table or light box is a wonderful way to examine the glass up close to discover any bubbles, lettering or maker's marks. A free-standing magnifying glass might be another great tool for examining your finds. A 30X or 40X magnification is ideal and can be purchased inexpensively. One of the best ways to determine what a piece of glass is from is by looking for manufacturing signs. Bottle or jar bases can offer clues as to the age of the glass based on its shape.

Bottle bases in the 1820s had what is known as push up bases, which were largely used for wine, as the undesirable wine sediment would collect in the ring at the bottom. A pontil scar would be left on the base from a rod of glass that was blown by hand; those can date from the 1830s to 1870s. Some bottles will display a company's initials, a single letter, emblem, logo or trademark. Sometimes there may only be a sequence of numbers or even a bottle mold number, which may be difficult to identify without a reference or detailed research. If the piece was manufactured with a mold, you might be able to identify a seam in the glass; the thickness or design may help in identification.

Certain sea glass colors become bucket list items for collectors, as some are rarer than others. The most common found colors are white/clear, brown/caramel and Kelly green, due to the mass production and abundance of soda, tonic, seltzer and beer bottles. The color green is made by adding iron, chromium or copper to the molten glass mixture during the manufacturing process. Green glass became more widely used in the seventeenth century, primarily for wine and alcohol, and a good rule of thumb is that the darker the green, the older the glass is. In the nineteenth century, mineral water was bottled in green glass, and there were several mineral springs in New England. Lime green glass is mostly connected to soda bottles that were

Left: Tiny beach-found treasures include a clay pipe, porcelain cup handle, tile, sea brick, pottery handles and other odds and ends.

Below: A weathered bottleneck rests among sea glass and seaweed.

Above: Bottle mold numbers can be found on some shards of glass. A closer look at the bottom can sometimes reveal a year or even a manufacturer name.

Right: All that remains of this old bottle is the frosted bottom.

Glass rings that have broken off bottles are a rare and exciting find.

mass produced in the twentieth century. White or clear glass comes from everyday items like dairy bottles, mason jars, medicine jars, windows and clear or crystal dinnerware. Brown bottles protected their content from harmful ultraviolet rays. Brown bottles that were used for beer would have identification stamps on them so that the bottles could be returned and reused. Brown glass snuff bottles were common and contained a type of powdered tobacco mixed with aromatic herbs.

Colors like seafoam green, dark green, lime green, amber and light blue are a little rarer. Lavender or light purple glass gets its color from the manganese that was added during the manufacturing process to keep the clear glass from discoloration. The age of this glass is from the late 1800s to the very early 1900s. Over time, as this glass is exposed to the ultraviolet rays from the sun, it will slowly start to turn lavender. Some collectors will continue to put this glass under the sun to bring out more of the purple color. Cobalt and cornflower blue are favorites of collectors and are less often seen tumbling across beaches. The beaches that surround Boston Harbor are often a good place to discover cobalt blue shards. Darker blues come from milk of magnesia, Vicks, Noxzema and perfume bottles. Olive green, teal, aqua, pink, yellow and gray prove to be more elusive. The rarest pair of colors is orange and red, as it was expensive to produce; either gold or copper would have been added to create the color. Sometimes these rare colors came from automobile lights or boat navigation lights. Black sea glass is always an exciting find because its true color is revealed with a light. Sometimes referred to as pirate glass, the color may show as green, brown or dark purple and can date back to the eighteenth or nineteenth century.

Many beachcombers get excited about sea pottery and love to delve into identifying their finds. Sometimes the crazing, or the crackles seen on the surface of the piece, can tell the age because the top glazed layer slowly breaks under the stress of being tossed around the tides. Changes in temperature can also cause crazing to sea pottery. Some pieces of sea pottery can have an identifiable maker's mark (hallmark), pattern number or origin location. Transferware pottery dates to the late 1700s and 1800s and

Left: The deep, rich cobalt blue color of some glass comes from cobalt oxide or copper oxide that has been added to the hot, molten glass.

Right: A punt or a kick up in an old wine bottle was used to separate the sediment. It also acted like a weight for transporting the bottle, adding to its stability during shipment.

was created by transferring a detailed design from a copper plate onto the piece. Other pieces of pottery can sometimes be identified as spongeware, where the repeating design was created with pieces of cloth or sponge; these date between the 1850s and 1950s.

If you are looking to research your pottery and porcelain finds, there is a terrific book that was written by C. Jordan Thorn called *Handbook of Old Pottery & Porcelain Marks*, published by the Tudor Publishing Company of New York in 1947. There are approximately four thousand identified maker's marks and manufacturing stamps in the book, along with images, dates and locations. The book is well organized and features a section on the United States and marks from all over the world. Sitting down with your unidentified pieces and discovering them in this book is like traveling in time across the globe.

There are many guidelines and charts available with information about grading the quality of sea glass. Grade A–Jewelry Grade is considered pieces that are rounded with even frosting or sugaring on the surface with no chips, cracks or breaks. Grade B–Jewelry Grade is less rounded with a small chip,

Above, left: Sea glass comes in a variety of colors and thicknesses, which can often help determine its age.

Above, right: A shard of glass from a Pepsi bottle that dates to the 1940s/1950s.

Left: A shard from a 1950s glass measuring cup.

rough or shiny spot and perhaps an uneven frost or sugar. Craft Grade is irregular or odd-shaped glass with rough edges and/or chips. It can be easy to get caught up in grading sea glass, and people have a variety of personal preferences. Some people are happy to just have found a piece of glass, while other folks are more discerning about their choices. There are no rules or right or wrong answers to the choices you make about your glass.

If you find a piece of sea glass that appears to be an odd, almost bubbly shape, you may have found what is referred to as "bonfire glass." Bonfire glass is a fascinating find, where the original shape or color of the glass has been transformed by fire. Sometimes those fires come from beach or campfires or other events like a structure fire or brush fire. The heat of the flame melts the glass, creating bubbles or an uneven, melted surface. The glass will sometimes have sand, pebbles, stones or even other melted

Above: Shards, chips and pebbles from old crockery is often overlooked or left behind by sea glass searchers.

Left: A shard of wired safety glass, which was manufactured to prevent the glass from shattering in case of emergencies.

glass pieces embedded in it. That piece of bonfire glass then gets tumbled and worn by the waves and tides. Each piece is incredibly unique and is a product of complete transformation.

Developing an eye for discovering the origins of your sea glass or sea pottery can be exciting and fun. Popping over to your local thrift or antique shop and examining the glassware for sale is a terrific way of discovering glassware patterns and bottle designs. Shuffling through plates and teacups may surprise you when it comes to matching up pieces of pottery, earthenware, stoneware and porcelain. A few selected pieces might work well for displaying your finds, such as a blue willow bowl for matching sea pottery or an adorned cut glass candy dish for your decorative sea shards. While perusing antique shops, old catalogues and books on antique glass collecting can be purchased at reasonable prices and are a perfect addition to a reference library for your treasures. What makes researching pieces of glass particularly

intriguing in New England is the extensive history of glass manufacturing that the region has.

Portland, Maine, was home to the Portland Glass Company, which operated from 1863 to 1873 in a four-story brick building on Canal Street (now Commercial Street) along Portland Harbor. They claimed that their glass was superior to Parisian glass, and they outfitted many hotels in the region with their glassware. In 1866, they manufactured 976,000 pieces of glassware, 40,000 dozen crates of kerosene lamps and 100,000 ale, whiskey and wine glasses. Most of their pieces were clear, and they pressed over sixty different patterns, including their signature "tree of life" pattern. In their last year of operation, material costs had become quite expensive and the industry saw a downturn, so they closed. Some of their products can be seen in the Portland Museum of Art and at the Fifth Avenue Gallery of the Metropolitan Museum of Art in New York.

The New Bedford Museum of Glass is located at the historic Arnold Mansion, built in 1821, on County Street. New Bedford was once considered the art glass capital of the country, and the industry at its height employed 1,200 people. The museum has over seven thousand historic glass treasures in its collection. Throughout numerous exhibits, the museum highlights the local history of glassmaking. The Mount Washington Glass Company evolved into the Pairpoint Corporation in 1894, and it was known for popular, high-quality products. There is a large display of glowing uranium glass at the museum in addition to a gift shop full of glass creations. This is

Opposite: Crockery and brown pottery are abundant on New England beaches. This durable ceramic would provide watertight storage for salted meats, butter, grains and other foods that needed to stay cool and dry.

Above: Antique shops are among the best places for researching the many different origins of sea glass.

A closer look at the many patterns of cut decorative sea glass.

also a great place to do research, as it has an extensive reference library of books and research papers on the history of glass.

The New England Glass Company evolved out of the defunct Porcelain and Glass Manufacturing Company of East Cambridge, Massachusetts. They became one of the most successful and largest glass companies in the world for the better part of the nineteenth century. The weekly paper *Gleason's Pictorial Drawing Room Companion* did a feature on the company and said: "There is hardly a home from Maine to Louisiana which has not more or less of this excellent ware in domestic use. Every description of glassware, from a simple pressed glass wine glass to the most elaborately cut and richly plated, gilded, silvered and engraved glass is produced in a style of beauty and excellence unrivaled in the world." Advancements in the materials used to manufacture glass produced a decline in sales, and a decrease in their workforce caused the company to be taken over and eventually moved to Ohio, where it became known as Libbey Glass in 1888.

A man named Deming Jarves got his start in the business of glassmaking at the New England Glass Company, and after a visit to Sandwich, Massachusetts, he decided to open a glass factory there in 1825. He chose Sandwich because he felt there were enough natural resources to support the factory, like the sprawling woodland that would supply the glass blowing fires with fuel. Also, the abundant salt hay was used to pack the glass for shipment. Boston Harbor was also a close distance, which helped set up Jarves for success. The company did so well that they produced twenty-four tons of glass each week, which was shipped by boat and peddlers' wagons across the country. He had a 350-foot dock built, as well as other structures that supported transporting the finished goods. In 1858, Jarves had a dispute with the board of directors and started his own company, the Cape Cod Glass Works, which did not see the same success as the Boston and Sandwich Glass Works. Over the next fifty years, the fate of the company hung in the balance as it encountered a number of challenges. Finally, the company closed in 1908, and slowly the factory was dismantled. A plaque was put in place to commemorate the history of the factory. Over the years, pieces of glass from the factory have been pulled out of the salt marshes behind the factory site, which was referred to as Jarvesville.

In some historic texts, Sandwich is referred to as the "town that glass built" due to the thriving community it became. Laborers, glassblowers and artists from Europe put down roots in Sandwich while the industry thrived. Today, the Sandwich Historical Society operates the Sandwich Glass Museum, which collects, preserves and interprets the history of the town. Its mission is to relight the fires on the glass industry, which it does through glass-blowing experiments and exhibits of glass artifacts. It is the perfect place to visit to understand the manufacturing and use of glass in the nineteenth century. With thousands of pieces of glass on display, from nineteenth-century marbles to bottles, jars, plates and lamps, it is an

The Sandwich Glass Museum collects, preserves and interprets the history of the town of Sandwich, the oldest town on Cape Cod.

An old, bubbly blue blob of blown glass from the Sandwich Glass Factory.

118

ideal place for the sea glass collector to visit and learn about the history of glassmaking.

There are several sea glass festivals and expositions around the world each year, and taking the time to visit or participate in them is time well spent. There are opportunities to meet other beachcombers, view collections and learn more about future places to explore. There are often artists and creative folks selling and showing off their creations made from beach-found treasures. Some festivals will even have people on hand to help you identify your finds. Plus, while you're there, check out the local beaches, where you might find that special souvenir tumbling along the shore.

CHAPTER 10

DISPLAYS AND CRAFTING

J ars, bowls and bottles are an easy choice for cataloguing and displaying your collection. Setting them up on a windowsill where the natural light sets the glass aglow is a great way to enjoy your finds. A label on the bottom of the container can also include the collection information. Small LED fairy lights can be added to any bottle or jar to add a soft glow from the inside of the glass. Canning jars work quite well for sorting sea glass as well. A canning jar can be filled halfway with glass with a tea light placed on the top for an elegant display.

Printer trays or letterpress drawers are a perfect way to sort and display your finds, as they have multiple compartments that are often just the right size for beach finds. Museum putty can be used to adhere the glass to the drawer for display on the wall, or a piece of glass can be cut to go over the top for a tabletop display. Some collectors buy or build coffee table displays with glass tops so that they can arrange and view their finds easily.

Floating frames are a terrific way to appreciate the colors of your sea glass, as they allow the light to shine through them. The frames are affordable and easy to assemble. Placing the completed frames on a windowsill or near a natural light source is a perfect way to enjoy your treasures and perhaps even notice small details or designs in the glass.

Sea glass is an ideal treasure for jewelry makers, who can create bezels to showcase the piece's beauty. Other jewelry makers wire wrap their sea glass into pendants or charms to be worn. Another option jewelry makers will use is to drill holes into the glass with Dremel tools to create a hole to

Using vintage glass bottles to display your finds is a great way to tell the story of sea glass from beginning to end.

A sample of the author's collection of sea glass sorted into labeled bottles and jars.

use a loop or a bail to hang the sea glass. Embellishing the jewelry with the addition of seashells or even beach pebbles really brings the feel of the beach to the piece.

It almost seems as though sea glass is ready made for mosaics, glass art and tile artists, as it goes together rather easily. Mixing sea glass pieces with sea pottery is a fun way to get creative and create something truly unique. Mosaic trays, trivets, coasters and tabletops are a great way to show off and enjoy your collection at your fingertips. Some people have even created colorful backsplashes out of sea glass and tile.

Filling a jewelry box or treasure chest with sea glass, shells and driftwood is a terrific way to tell the story of your beachy adventures. You can continue to add your beach-found treasures and create many different layers. The treasure box might be a great way to stay connected to the sea in case you don't get to go exploring often. For a twist, you can always put sand in the box and mix in or hide some sea glass for a little ready-made mini adventure.

Another fun idea is to take the driftwood, stones and shells that you may have collected along with your sea glass and create fairy houses or gnome homes. You can use a piece of driftwood for the base and add

shells, dried mosses or seaweed to create a roof. You want to be sure that you are utilizing a strong glue, like E6000, to hold your creation together. These would look great displayed in gardens or among houseplants. Toss a few pieces in with an air plant, terrarium or in a succulent planter to add a special beachy touch.

Left: Sea glass is a terrific material for building whimsical fairy houses.

Opposite: The display of nineteenth-century pressed scent and perfume bottles at the Sandwich Glass Museum.

CHAPTER 11

THE FUTURE OF SEA GLASS

While it is true that nowadays more people than ever are collecting sea glass, the last piece has not been plucked from the waves just yet. In chatting with divers, lobstermen and others who spend a lot of time on and in the water, it is clear there is still quite a bit of glass and tumbled treasure to find in the sea. A lot of sea glass is embedded in rocks and the floor of the ocean itself, and sometimes it takes just the right conditions to set it loose into the tides.

The use of glass vessels, bottles and containers has sharply dropped over the years with more widespread use of plastic, recyclable and reusable materials. This is wonderful for the environment and has clearly helped to clean up polluted beaches. Some beaches even prohibit glass containers from being used. Activism for beach cleanups and wetland preservation affects the availability of sea glass in some areas; however, there is so much New England shoreline still to be explored. There are many beaches that are now open for exploration that were dangerously toxic only twenty-five or thirty years ago, when collecting sea glass would have been hazardous to your health and safety. No one can truly tell when the last piece of sea glass will be collected, and because of that, for many, the hunt will continue.

CONCLUSION

Rolling home, rolling home
Rolling home across the sea
Rolling home to old New England
Rolling home dear land to thee.
—traditional sea shanty from the 1800s

While there are many places to explore and enjoy in this book, use these ideas as a launching pad for further explorations of other locations that you might find on the way or nearby. There is a lifetime of adventures to be had out there along the New England coastline, and you might end up finding a quiet beach off the beaten path that no one has discovered or combed through yet. Giving yourself time to explore and getting to know the area can prove to be quite fruitful with some patience.

Also, remember, there is something special about collecting sea glass and beach-worn treasures that transcends the finds themselves. The symbolism and inspiration of finding something that has been broken, discarded or lost and has been shaped by time and tide into something beautiful has its own magical appeal. A simple beach outing can help you unplug from the stresses of the mundane world, and having a focus while there can be quite healing to a troubled mind. We sometimes find that we can get away from it all while walking the shore and listening to the waves in their beautiful rhythmic cycle. Some people describe their explorations as almost spiritual experiences while they are alone on a beach with the sounds of the sea.

Have you ever noticed how many different shades of blue the ocean can be while looking across the water? Or how the sun sparkles like thousands of precious gems floating back and forth in the currents? The waves roll away but always return to the shore, sometimes soft and gentle, while other times wild and full of power. The salty spray can playfully cool us on a hot day, and watery whirlpools sometimes swirl with bubbling foam as if inside an invisible cauldron. Our imagination might visualize the mythological god Poseidon waving his trident, orchestrating the motion and conditions of the tides.

Try to allow your beach explorations to be adventurous, mysterious and even mystical while gazing on the never-ending sea. There are so many people who live landlocked and wish to see the ocean and explore all its shorelines have to offer. When you pick up a little treasure tossed by the waves, you are holding a piece of history, an unmistakable link to the past and sometimes a mystery. Each discovery is a gift, and the perfect conditions had to occur for you to pick it up at the right place and right time. May you have fair winds and following seas in your travels, and I wish you unforgettable adventures by the shore to fill your soul as well as your pockets.

BIBLIOGRAPHY

Boston Evening Transcript. "The Lighthouse of Minot's Ledge." May 2, 1851, 1.

Brooks, Charles Timothy. "Aquidneck: A Poem, Pronounced on the Hundredth Anniversary of the Incorporation of the Redwood Library Company, Newport, R.I. August 24, 1847. With Other Commemorative Pieces." C. Burnett Jr., 1848.

Gibbons, John. "Flashback: American Vogues in Porcelain Since Colonial Days." *Collectors Weekly*, April 16, 2010.

Harper's New Monthly Magazine 9, no. 2 (February 1851).

Historic and Architectural Resources of Jamestown, Rhode Island. Providence: Rhode Island Historical Preservation Commission, 1995.

MacIsaac, Kimberly E. *Peaks Island: Past and Present.* Thomaston: Maine Authors Publishing, 2021.

New England Historical Society. "Sandwich Glass Builds a Cape Cod Town." newenglandhistoricalsociety.com/sandwich-glass-builds-a-cape-cod-town.

Schwartz, George. "Digging Up Salem's Golden Age: Ceramic Use Among the Merchant Class." Chipstone. Chipstone.org/article.php/480/Ceramics-in-America-2011.

Troost-Cramer, Kathleen. *True Tales of Life & Death at Fort Adams.* Charleston, SC: The History Press, 2013.

ABOUT THE AUTHOR

New England's Mystery Maven, Roxie Zwicker has been entertaining the locals, visitors from away and curious souls since 1994. Her company, New England Curiosities, located in Portsmouth, New Hampshire, has been offering award-winning tours, presentations and special events since 2002 based on New England folklore and mysterious history. Roxie's TV appearances include *New Hampshire Chronicle*, New England Cable News, the History Channel and the Travel Channel. Roxie is a published author of several books that delve into the region's history, legends and lore. Her extensive collection of sea glass and beach-found treasures takes up an entire room in her house. *Wicked Curious Radio* is Roxie's podcast, available on all major podcast platforms, and her website can be found at www.newenglandcuriosities.com.